MIRACLES

BY THE

MOMENT

LARRY & TIZ HUCH

CHARISMA
HOUSE

permission of Tyndale House Publishers, Inc., Wheaton, IL 60189.
All rights reserved.

Visit the author's website at larryhuchministries.com.

Cataloging-in-Publication Data is on file with the Library of
Congress.
International Standard Book Number: 978-1-63641-106-4
E-book ISBN: 978-1-63641-107-1

Portions of this book were previously published by Whitaker
House as *No Limits, No Boundaries*, ISBN 978-1-60374-119-4,
copyright © 2009.

22 23 24 25 26 — 987654321
Printed in the United States of America

DEDICATIONS

I dedicate this book to Larry, my husband, my bashert-soul mate, the love of my life, and my best friend. Larry, for forty-six years you have been my greatest inspiration, motivation, fearless leader, teacher, world adventurer, and greatest hero! You have led me and our family with love, selflessness, unshakable faith, courage, vision, integrity, encouragement, positivity, prayers, compassion, generosity, tireless work, humor, and joy. You continue to astound me and make me proud every day in every way. Thank you for being you and always leading us to the mountaintops. Our best is yet to come!

I also dedicate this book to my kids and their spouses: Anna, Brandin, Luke, Jen, and Katie. You amaze me! You are my answered prayers and dreams come true. I've seen you not only rise to but above the challenges. You've been sources of faith, prayers, strength, encouragement, help, TLC, joy, and leadership to me, Dad, each other, the sugars, our congregation, and the world. I love and am so proud of each of you and love watching your light shine bright!

I dedicate this book to my "sugars" (grandkids): Asher, Judah, Aviva, and Lion. You fill my life with joy, love, fun, laughter, and inspiration! I've watched you grow, mature, and stay strong in the midst of the storms. I know you have a great future and destiny from the Lord and He will use your lives to bring inspiration, light, hope, and leadership to the world around you. I love you and am proud of you!

Also, I dedicate this book to my mom and dad, who have always been my greatest influences and models of love and family. As you watch from heaven, know that you are forever in my heart, soul, family, and life!

I dedicate this book to staff, friends, extended families, colleagues, congregations, stream families, ministry partners, synagogues, rabbis, pastors, and prayer partners. Your love, prayers, and support make it possible for us to continue making a difference for the Lord.

Finally, I dedicate this book to my God, my Lord, my Salvation, my Redeemer, my healer, my breath, my King, my everything!

—TIZ HUCH

꧂

I dedicate this book to my incredible, beautiful wife, Tiz! You are the love of my life, my best friend, and my greatest gift from God. For forty-six years you have been by my side, my greatest supporter, my deepest inspiration, and my closest ally and partner in every area of our lives. You are truly the most loving, genuine, compassionate, dedicated, kind, generous, courageous, strong, wise, faith-filled, positive, powerful, hardworking, and godly woman I have known. I am honored to call you my wife and share my journey with you. These past few years have been tough, but you have been tougher! You have pressed through these attacks on Lion's and your health as a warrior and a champion. You've been an inspiration to us all and held your head high in faith, grace, joy, and class. Your faith and trust in God and His promises have been unwavering and an inspiration to me, our family, and the world. Most importantly, you made it through and are totally healed, restored, and more beautiful than ever. Our greatest days are ahead!

I also dedicate this book to my kids and their spouses: Anna, Brandin, Luke, Jen, and Katie. I'm so thankful for and proud of you. Through this journey you have each risen above and beyond the challenges we've faced into new levels of faith, courage, strength, commitment, compassion, love, and spiritual leadership. Despite our own issues, you continued to pour out to others, and you've been such a great help and encouragement to Mom, me, and each other. You are champs!

And I dedicate this book to my "sugars" (grandkids): Asher, Judah, Aviva, and Lion. You are the joy of my life! I am so proud of each of you and so excited to see your futures and destinies evolve.

May you each love and follow the Lord with all your heart, love each other, love people, love Israel, and remember God's promise "I will bless those who bless [Israel]" (Gen. 12:3). We are blessed to be a blessing!

—LARRY HUCH

CONTENTS

ACKNOWLEDGMENTS

WE WOULD LIKE to give special thanks, love, appreciation, and blessings to the Texas Oncology-Presbyterian Cancer Center, as well as Dr. Dustin Manders, the nurses, the staff, the chemo center, and the support teams.

We thank the Cook Children's Medical Center Oncology Department, along with the doctors, nurses, staff, technology, chaplains, and support teams.

We'd also like to thank all our wonderful family, friends, staff, congregations, stream family, and ministry partners, as well as Christians and Jews from all over the world, who joined together in surrounding our family with love, support, faith, and prayers. Much thanks, love, and blessings!

Above all and most importantly we give thanks, glory, and honor to God Almighty, the God of Abraham, Isaac, and Jacob. We will declare your love, goodness, blessings, and miracles all the days of our lives!

INTRODUCTION
LARRY HUCH

I shall not die, but live, and declare the works of the LORD.
—PSALM 118:17

I will bless those who bless [Israel].
—GENESIS 12:3

I'VE BEEN TO Israel thirty-nine times, but one of the most exciting times was when the United States Embassy officially relocated to Jerusalem on May 14, 2018. I was in Jerusalem for the moving of the embassy, and after the ceremony we met with some friends for dinner. Though it was getting late, one of our friend's phone rang, and it was his wife.

She said, "I know it's late. It's almost too late to call you, but I really felt like the Lord wanted me to say something to Pastor Larry."

Her husband said, "Well, he's sitting right here." He turned to me and said, "My wife wants to talk to you."

I got on the phone, and his wife said, "God told me to tell you this. The lion will roar from Jerusalem."

I was thinking, "Well, we're in Jerusalem. We just moved the embassy. This is awesome. The lion will roar from Jerusalem."

I said, "OK. Great. Thanks." Then I hung up the phone.

About three minutes later, my son Luke called me and said, "Dad, we need you guys to pray. We're taking Lion to the hospital."

Lion, who at that time was seven months old, is our grandson. I said, "What's wrong?"

Luke replied, "We don't know, but something's wrong." He has been crying uncontrollably, has a fever, and seems as if he's in a lot of pain. And we can't console him. We prayed together on the phone for Lion and for the doctors to have wisdom and guidance as to what was wrong with him.

We hung up the phone, and I said another prayer for Lion.

A day or two later when I was flying back to the States, I found myself mulling over the message "The lion will roar from Jerusalem."

The medical testing process began immediately and went on for several weeks. Luke, Jen, and Lion had been checked into the Children's Hospital because of the severity of Lion's symptoms and the extensiveness of the tests. Through the process of elimination, the options of causes became more narrow, serious, and alarming. The waiting time between the tests and getting the results is very unnerving. We all stayed positive and hopeful and stood in faith for God's promises of healing. Finally the day came to get the results from the last and biggest tests and spinal tap. Tiz and I and our family met at our church with our staff, leaders, and friends to have a time of prayer over Lion.

Confident that we were going to get a good report, we went to the hospital to meet with Luke, Jen, Lion, and the doctor in their room. As we knocked and walked in, we saw that the doctor, several nurses, and the hospital chaplain were already in the room. The doctor was sitting down, leaning in to speak with Luke and Jen, who were both sobbing. You know when the chaplain is present, something's up. Baby Lion was crying uncontrollably as Luke held him tightly in his arms. Luke was weeping into Lion's baby blanket. Jen was wrapped tightly around Luke and Lion, sobbing hysterically.

As we all stood there stunned and in shock, Luke looked up at me, shook his head, and whispered through his tears, "It's not good, Dad." Immediately we all quickly gathered around them, giving hugs amid the tears. The doctor introduced himself to us all as the director of the oncology program at the Children's Hospital. Then he compassionately went on to tell us that the bone marrow test showed conclusively that Lion had a rare, severe, life-threatening form of leukemia. Tiz and I share more of Lion's story in the pages that follow, but suffice it to say, we were in shock and disbelief. Within a few weeks we had gone from testing for ear infections and stomach viruses to leukemia? Suddenly we are discussing not how long a simple infection might last but statistics of how long a rare form of leukemia might last and affect Lion's entire life and future. Surely there must be some kind of mistake here! My heart broke as I watched my own grown son, Jen, and family weep in emotional agony as we watched baby Lion weep in physical agony.

The shock waves of the news were soon overshadowed by the questions and uncertainties of what lay ahead. Today's news was just the beginning of endless information, statistics, treatment plans, life adjustments, and massive to-do lists and responsibilities ahead. The heaviness in the room was intense as reality set in. It felt as if our world had been shattered and our foundation had been ripped out from under our feet. We prayed as a family in faith for God's supernatural healing and wholeness; for His direction and wisdom upon the medical teams; and for God's strength, peace, and equipping for Luke, Jen, and Lion through this journey. As we prayed, I kept hearing the words "The lion will roar from Jerusalem." And I kept hearing the scripture "I will bless those who bless [Israel]." That verse marks the time when God started the nation of Israel through a promise He made to Abram:

> I will make you a great nation; I will bless you and make your name great; and you shall be a blessing. I will bless those who bless you, and I will curse him who curses you; and in you all the families of the earth shall be blessed.
>
> —Genesis 12:2–3

As we went through this trial with Lion, we were going to need to hold on to God's promises for blessings on his life. Then less than a year later the doctors ran tests that showed Tiz had stage 3 ovarian cancer.

We kept holding on as a family. We kept holding on to God's Word in Genesis 12:3 when He said, "I will bless those who bless you."

We've invested so much of our hearts and our ministry into Israel and made friends with Jews around the world. I was in awe when thousands of Christians and thousands of Jewish people from Israel contacted us.

One said, "I'm down at the Western Wall right now. I'm praying."

Another said, "We're going to our synagogue right now. We are praying." One Jewish brother summed it up when he said, "We are asking God for your blessing, for your merit, that God will heal your grandson and God will heal your wife because of your merit of standing with the nation of Israel."

I know there are so many biblical reasons to stand with the nation of Israel. We can trust that almighty God will always keep His Word. God will bless those who bless the nation of Israel. I sincerely believe God double blessed us and caused our healing journey to end the way it did because we love and bless God's nation, Israel, and His people, the Jews.

Maybe you need a miracle in your home or your family. Maybe you need a miracle in your business or your health, like my family did. Our God is no respecter of persons. I know without a shadow of a doubt that God worked a miracle for Lion and Tiz. Everywhere we go now we tell our story. Let's begin with what my dear wife, Tiz, recounts about the day of her cancer diagnosis. Just remember—our story starts out rough, but it gets better and ends with incredible miracles and victories for both Lion and Tiz. Both are totally healthy and cancer-free today!

CHAPTER 1

"I HAVE BAD NEWS"
TIZ HUCH

HOLOCAUST SURVIVOR ELIE Wiesel is often quoted as saying, "Whoever survives a test, whatever it may be, must tell the story. That is his duty."[1] Larry and I survived a severe test, and we feel it our duty to tell you our story.

The doctor entered the examining room with my medical files in his hand. He introduced himself to me, my husband, and our two daughters, Anna and Katie, then sat down.

"I'm sorry, but I have some bad news," he said as he leaned forward in his chair. "Your CT scan and ultrasound reveal that you have aggressive, stage 3 ovarian cancer."

I froze. Did he just say stage 3 cancer?

The doctor continued. "Unfortunately, it's spread extensively throughout your female organs and abdomen."

When a person has a near-death experience, they say their whole past life flashes before their eyes. I had a similar experience, but I didn't see my past flash before my eyes. I saw my future—without me in it.

I glanced at Larry and our girls. No one moved.

The doctor took out his pen to jot down a few notes as he explained the details of what he saw on my test results.

"Mrs. Huch, you will need immediate emergency surgery, followed by six months of heavy chemotherapy..."

The doctor's voice faded, and the room disappeared down a long tunnel. I couldn't hear anything else he said. Images flashed before my eyes. In what seemed to play like movie clips, I saw

1

my family at my funeral standing over me as I lay in a coffin, crying and consoling one another. I saw images of Larry trying to carry on in life, family, and ministry without me. I saw visions of our daughter Katie getting married without me being there. I saw all my kids having more kids. I saw my grandkids growing up, graduating, getting married, and having their own kids— all without me in the picture. I saw images of our lives, church, and ministries evolving without me. I saw pictures of my sister and brother and their families gathered together with everyone present except me. This all flashed through my brain in a matter of seconds.

The doctor continued speaking, only a few feet away from me, but my tunnel vision made him look a hundred yards away. His lips were moving, but I couldn't hear a word he was saying. I saw my future through the lens of this potentially deadly cancer diagnosis, and I was horrified.

Out of the corner of my eye I saw Larry, Anna, and Katie. All three were staring—shocked. Everything within me wanted to jump up, rush over, and grab them and console them as a mom and wife. But I was frozen and could not even turn my head to make eye contact with them. All of this seemed like hours but really was only a few seconds. I tried to focus my attention on what the doctor was saying.

"Due to the severity of the cancer," he said, "I don't want to waste valuable time scheduling a biopsy or other tests that are normal procedures."

I was thankful we had an expert in the field of oncology but stunned when he said this type of cancer was fast spreading and had already advanced to many of my organs. He cleared his calendar and said he would do surgery on me in a couple of days then start me on chemotherapy for the next four to six months.

Suddenly I snapped out of my numbness as he said, "We will use the strongest kind of chemo that exists at the maximum level possible. It will work extremely fast and hard. It's not going to be easy on you. You'll lose all your hair all over your body within the first few weeks…"

Those are the words that broke through the daze and the scenes playing out in my head. I gasped and broke out sobbing. My girls and Larry grabbed me in hugs and tears of love, horror, and support. The doctor paused and gave us a few seconds to catch our breath before continuing.

The words that the chemo would make all my hair fall out hit me like a lightning bolt, not from a vanity point but from a reality point that I was losing my "life" as I knew it. If someone you love is facing chemo, it's important to identify with their loss in the broader sense of the word. My life, my family, my health, and my future had just been ripped from me. I felt like I had been blindsided and hit by a semitruck. The diagnosis of "the big C" is beyond comprehension. In the natural realm, without medical help or miracles, it can be a death sentence. Thoughts of the far-reaching effects of cancer, major surgery, and chemo overwhelmed me—frightened me.

How would this all play out? Cancer, major surgery, recovery, chemo…

Again, thoughts of the future paraded through my mind: "What will my life actually be like? What will I look like? Will I be able to continue working and go to church, have a normal life? How will my family deal with this? Am I going to be feeble? Will the chemo actually work? Then what? What about all our commitments, plans, and calendar schedules?"

I know these same thoughts, feelings, and questions were racing through Larry's, Anna's, and Katie's minds as we all hugged each other close and caught our breath. What was our future going to look like?

Immediately my thoughts turned to little Lion, our grandson. My diagnosis came about a year after our seven-month-old grandbaby had been diagnosed with a rare form of leukemia.

BABY LION

In 2018, our son Luke and his wife, Jen, had their first child, a beautiful baby boy. They knew God had given him His name—Lion. We were all absolutely ecstatic over Lion and so thankful for the blessings and joy within our family. We were actually giddy about him! He was the happiest, most handsome little newborn we could imagine.

When he was seven months old, Lion suddenly woke up in the middle of the night screaming inconsolably and shaking with a fever. The fever wouldn't break permanently, and our dear little grandson seemed to be in pain. After several doctor and ER visits, Lion was admitted to the children's hospital, where they began a series of intensive testing to find the source. Luke and Jen stayed in the room with Lion night and day, never leaving his side.

Several weeks later the physician who is the director of children's oncology at the hospital came to tell them the results. Our whole family was there with them. He told Luke and Jen how sorry he was to tell them this, but their tests were conclusive.

He explained that Lion had a very rare and aggressive type of leukemia. His bone marrow test showed that nearly 90 percent of his spinal fluid had leukemia cells present. They had researched extensively but could not find one known case in the world of an infant surviving this kind of cancer. It is so rare in infants that little is even known. There are many more variables, potential complications, and risks to treatments at such a young age of development, with no guarantees that treatment would even work. They would only know as it went along.

We sat stunned as the doctor briefed us and laid out statistics of survival and long-term projections. He promised they would do their best but gave very little hope for or chance of Lion's survival. As a family, our world was shaken to the core.

Under this doctor's guidance, the hospital moved Lion to the oncology area on the fifth floor, where he was prepped to start chemotherapy immediately—a chemo treatment that would last two years. Out of those two years, he lived on the oncology floor with his parents for a total of six months. Can you imagine being a new parent and living with your new baby on a cancer floor among other gravely ill children for months at a time? It's hard to comprehend even for those who have had to endure it.

Luke and Jen never left the hospital for the first two months of treatment. Then they had to spend the extended periods of time "living" at the hospital throughout the two years of treatment. Their dreams of raising their baby boy and the joy of his first year of life was suddenly reduced to seeing him in a hospital bed, with a dozen tubes plugged into a port to his heart. Their days and nights were jam-packed with nonstop tests, blood work, meds, temperature readings, and so on. Baby Lion was poked, prodded, and worked on nonstop. Being given chemo created many additional issues and dangers that had to be continually monitored and dealt with. There was so much information to absorb, process, and deal with. There were so many tears to hold back. There were so many responsibilities to step up to.

It was hard for Larry and me to watch Luke and Jen walk through all this. Instead of taking their baby boy in a stroller through the park, they rolled his crib down the hall to go for another spinal tap or more tests. Instead of enjoying Lion's first year in their own home, their life with Lion was reduced to a tiny room on the fifth floor of the children's hospital. Instead of a swing set in their lush green backyard, their window overlooked the hospital's giant concrete parking lot.

As you can imagine, keeping faith in God and His promises doesn't come easily when your entire world is filled with children in various stages of cancer. It is heartbreaking to see parents and families sobbing in the hallways, grieving for their sick or dying child. During our visits with Lion, we all witnessed doctors and nurses consoling parents as they gave them devastating news. And, worst of all, we met families whose little ones lost their battle against cancer.

Cancer doesn't just try to rob you of your health or predict your death. It tries to rob you of your actual ongoing life. For me, it felt like being violated, like I was a victim of an assault, battery, and robbery. Cancer tries to rob not only the person with the diagnosis, but the families and friends and other people in your life. It tries to rob you all of your future and destiny together.

SET YOUR MIND ON THE MIRACLE

There were so many prayers to pray and miracles to believe for, so many opportunities for God to show Himself strong and powerful on our behalf, such big challenges, such an even bigger God! Luke, Jen, and Lion had no choice but to live in the hospital, although they were allowed to go home for a few short periods of time. On day one, they were told they could only go home after Lion finished the first phase of his treatment plan and his blood counts were in a normal place. Luke and Jen said it's an interesting place to be in, stuck in a position where you have no end date. It makes you really look for the light of God in every moment.

They chose to live every day cherishing the moments they had together, building new memories and reaching regular baby milestones, no matter the circumstances. They activated their faith through prayer, reading the Word, speaking scriptures daily over their family, and proclaiming all God's promises for their lives. The very same day Lion was diagnosed with cancer, Luke and Jen posted on Facebook that Lion was healed, he would live, and he would thrive, because they knew you have to set your mind on the miracle. In fact, that became their motto. They would not allow this circumstance to define Lion's destiny, as they knew God was in the center of it all. They stood together and built each other up by looking for miracles by the moment with the support of their extended family and church.

Lion had one more big test to undergo that would show whether the chemo was working and reveal even more about his condition in the days ahead. We all knew Lion was healed, but we were looking for the doctors to give us a good report. We walked through the valley, praying and believing for the victory every day. We called on God to provide the answer we were looking for, the kind of answer only He can provide—the final report that Lion was healed and cancer-free.

VICTORY IS SWEET

Lion went through the final test in phase 1 of his treatment—a second bone marrow test. This test would be the moment of truth as to whether the chemo and treatment were going to work on Lion. Remember, his previous bone marrow test showed nearly 90 percent of his spinal fluid contained leukemia cells.

The following day, the doctor shared the results of the testing. He said, "I have some really good news for you. Lion is cancer-free!" Wow! In less than two months of chemo treatment Lion was cancer-free and released to go home! This was a grand slam! Not only was our family ecstatic, but the doctors and nurses were astounded at these results. Lion's medical team members are some of the best in the world and have access to the highest levels of treatment and best facilities available. They all, without a doubt, admitted that there had to have been "help from above" to see these amazing results and this huge victory!

He said Lion still needed to complete his two years of chemo, so there was still more work to do and more extended periods of time to be spent in clinic and hospital treatment, but this part of the plan was definitely working and bringing better-than-expected results. We will never forget that day. We cried, praised, and shouted, "True miracles happened here!"

Lion experienced many miracles during his treatment—results and miracles we were told his doctors hadn't seen in their combined 150 years' experience! We did everything we possibly could in the natural realm of medicine, but we saw God go beyond that and put His super to our natural! It was such a blessing seeing the doctors and nurses so encouraged and infused with hope at Lion's victories and successes. On the day of his final release to go home, they held a little celebration party. They told Luke and Jen how much this victory meant to them in the midst of so much hardship and sadness that they see. Through tears they said, "We needed to see a win. Lion has made believers out of us all!"

Lion and I both experienced "miracles by the moment"—there are so many in Lion's testimony that Luke and Jen have talked about sharing them all in a book of their own. But the bottom line is that Lion was healed, and he is alive and thriving! Now Lion is nearly five years old. Knowing the level of life-threatening challenges he faced keeps us thanking God every day for the greater levels of life-giving miracles God poured out on baby Lion and our family.

What kind of miracle are you believing for? If God can work miracles to this degree for baby Lion, He can do them for you too!

FAITH PICTURES THE FUTURE WITH GOD IN IT

I want to share with you a saying I've taught for many years. I hope this will help you through whatever challenges you are facing in your season of life right now:

Fear grips us when we picture our future through the lens of the world's circumstances, challenges, and predictions *without* God in the picture. But faith, hope, and peace arise when we picture our future through the lens of the Word's promises, faith, and miraculous power *with* God in the picture.

Larry and I want to build your faith for your miracle as we tell you our story. We walked together *with* God in the picture after Lion's diagnosis in 2018 and then my diagnosis in 2019. We are believing together by faith that God's presence and God's promises will spill over onto you until you absorb them with the absolute certainty and faith that He loves you and you can trust Him completely.

This journey has been filled with miracles by the moment,

from those enormous in size to the tiniest details. God met us in every realm, in every issue that arose, and in every step of the way. There was a process we walked through together with our Lord, and we want you to benefit from that process so you will know how to deal with your situation in the natural, emotional, and spiritual realms. This journey wasn't over and done within just a few weeks or months or in just one prayer session. Deuteronomy 33:25 tells us, "As your days, so shall your strength be." This has been absolutely true for me and my family every moment of every day. Over the course of navigating extremely stormy seas, my Lord has calmed and carried us through it all.

Our journey has been unlike anything we have ever faced before in our family or ministry. In another sense, though, it has been *just* like anything we have ever gone through before. Although the challenges were greater, they were not greater than our God! Although they were far different from anything before, our God is exactly the same God yesterday, today, and forever.

Although the pit was deeper, God's grace and love were deeper still. Although this has been an unfamiliar, inconsistent journey, our God has been as familiar and consistent as He has always been.

STARS SHINE BRIGHTEST IN THE DARKEST SKIES

As an art lover and wannabe artist, I know that the way to create dimension and depth in a painting is to contrast light with darkness. One of my favorite paintings is of sunlight reflecting off a bright orange flower contrasted against a deep blue sky. The flowers seem to glow and jump off the canvas in vivid contrast. We see this in nature itself. Picture a sunset with glowing, fiery colors of orange, yellow, and pink lit up against the darkening, blue-gray evening skies. Everyone knows that the stars shine the brightest when the night skies are the darkest.

If we don't paint the picture and let people know how dark and difficult these past few years have been, there will be no true appreciation for how radiantly God has shined His miracles into our lives. The same way the incredible brightness of stars is magnified against the intense darkness of night, so are God's miracles magnified against the darkness of the times we faced.

Our intention in telling these stories is not to glorify what we have gone through but to glorify God's love, care, and power in getting us through it all. Our purpose in writing openly about this journey is not to bring attention to ourselves but to bring attention to our God and hope to others who are walking through life's challenges.

Having said that, hold onto your hope! All our stories shared here turn out for the good! Lion and I are both completely healed and cancer-free—whole, healthy, and doing fantastic. We are both on the other side in the happy-ending phase of our journeys, thank the Lord! Our hope is to encourage you in your journey. We made it through, and so can you. What the Lord has done for us, He can do for you too.

Daily we declare, "I shall not die, but live, and declare the works of the LORD" (Ps. 118:17).

To borrow a term from an old cowboy movie, we're going to reveal "the good, the bad, and the ugly." Our intention is to be honest and forthright about the challenges, big and small, that we faced. We want you to know how we rose up above those challenges and how God met us at each point of our needs with His miraculous help. We pray that the opening of our hearts will bring hope to your heart and lead you to the Lord's love, grace, and miracles by the moment!

CHAPTER 2

WHEN YOU NEED A MIRACLE
LARRY HUCH

WHERE DO YOU go when you need a miracle from God? In the previous chapter, Tiz described in some detail one of the darkest days of our lives. We were suddenly cast into the dark abyss of the big C we all dread—cancer. What do you do when the doctor says your wife needs surgery within a few days or she could die? We were planning an extended trip to Israel. Our calendar was packed with places we needed to be, messages to be preached, and people we wanted to meet.

Perhaps Satan has stolen your health or your finances or is working in underhanded ways to steal from you or divide your family. I want to encourage you right now to believe with us that our God is a God of miracles! So we return to my original question: Where do *you* go when you need a miracle from God?

If I need a miracle, I want my wife, Tiz, to pray for me! In fact, email us your miracle need at contact@larryhuchministries.com, and Tiz and I and our prayer team will pray for you too. Tiz prays so intently for people wherever we go in ministry. I've always said that she can pray and get people filled with the baptism of the Holy Spirit quicker than anyone I know. Looking back, I know without a doubt that the Lord put our lives together. I never could have accomplished what I have in my own life without Tiz.

OUR COMMITMENT TO BLESS ISRAEL

Tiz and I are wholeheartedly committed to restoring the church to its Judeo-Christian roots. By God's grace and the support and donations of our congregation, stream family, and television partners, I've had the honor of speaking at the Israeli Knesset, and Tiz and I together humbly received awards from the Knesset Social Welfare Lobby for giving toward the needs of the Jewish people in Israel, helping build hospitals, purchasing nine ambulances (mobile ICU vehicles) that save thousands of lives, feeding and caring for precious Holocaust survivors, and many other ongoing projects. For nearly ten years we have worked with the Israeli government agency Keren Hayesod to raise funds to bring Jewish people from around the world to *aliyah*, which means immigration to Israel. Many are from nations where they faced heavy and life-threatening anti-Semitism, persecution, or the ravages of war.

Recently, due to the Russian invasion of Ukraine, we helped to rescue, transport, and settle over thirty thousand Ukrainian people in Israel. As I write these words, Tiz, Katie, and I have just returned from Israel, where we toured one of the absorption centers that transition these Ukrainian families into Israeli life and welcomed a planeload of 160 Ethiopian Jews immigrating into Israel. I also had the incredible privilege of receiving the John Henry Patterson Guardian of Zion Award, given for the first time ever, from Keren Hayesod (Friends of Israel) and the Israeli government for our support of all these critical, life-saving projects. We were honored in a special event by Israeli President Isaac Herzog; Mickey Levy, speaker of the Knesset; and leaders from around the world for fulfilling Bible prophecy and building bridges between Christians and Jews, efforts only made possible by the generous support of our faithful friends, congregation, and partners.

From Israel I flew directly to São Paulo, Brazil, to speak at an event where nearly five million people from all over the world marched in the streets, worshipping, praising, praying, and celebrating the unity of Christians and Jews. History is in the making! There is a powerful wave of God's Spirit sweeping across the world with signs, wonders, and miracles following! God is demonstrating His love and power to His people and to the world. As the evil influences are rising up in the world, our God is rising up in greater force, dominion, and power! Don't live in fear; live in the boldness of our God!

I tell you these things not just to explain what we do but to share our calling and the passion and focus of our lives, family, and ministries. We live on the foundation that we are blessed to be a blessing.

The incredible significance of this award from Keren Hayesod is that it marks the partnership and relationship forged between us as Christians and our Jewish brothers and sisters in the land of Israel. We know without a doubt that the miracles and blessings we have seen in Lion's and Tiz's lives have a direct link to our dedication to be an active blessing to the nation and people of Israel. This is a foundational truth that shows how we live in the continual flow of God's blessings and miracles. We get up every morning and ask the Lord what He is doing in the world that day and how He wants us to be part of it. We pray, listen, and obey.

The greatest way to receive God's miracles and blessings is by helping to be a miracle and blessing to others. The best way to get your own prayers answered is to be part of answering someone else's prayers. We are blessed to be a blessing!

I mentioned this in the introduction, but it bears repeating here. God made it clear to Abraham that He will bless those who bless Israel.

> I will bless those who bless you, and I will curse him who curses you; and in you all the families of the earth shall be blessed.
>
> —GENESIS 12:3

This is foundational in the Word of God from the beginning and continues until today. The Hebrew word *avot* means "fathers," and it is the term used for one of the sixty-three volumes of the Mishnah, which discusses all areas of Jewish law. The *Avot* is devoted to Jewish values, morals, and ethics and is thus called "Ethics of the Fathers," as these teachings provide the foundational principles upon which all the other teachings are built. They are the "father" of all the other Torah teachings. In ancient Hebrew teachings, the beginning of a thing is the most important aspect because how something begins determines how it continues and, ultimately, finishes.[1]

WE CHOOSE TO TRUST GOD DAILY

Tiz and I have been married more than forty-five years, and we have been pastoring together for the entirety of our marriage. Together we pioneered seven churches around the world, including two in Australia. We have preached salvation healing services and ministered in nearly every nation on earth. What a joy to see our Lord bring supernatural breakthroughs, healings, and miracles to people of many languages, skin colors, and nationalities. Our TV program and streaming services reach around the globe every day and bring the hope, life, and love of God to millions. It's a great honor and privilege to serve our God and see Him do such incredible things over the span of our lives together.

In the first year of our marriage, we decided that we were going to *choose* to trust God and His Word in every area of our lives. Determined, we pressed beyond the natural limitations of this world and into the unlimited promises and supernatural power of our God.

Tiz likes to say, "God will put His *super* into our *natural*." I like that.

That passionate pursuit to believe God has been our core foundation to this day. We have seen tens of thousands of people changed, healed, set free, and touched by life-altering miracles of every kind all over the world.

THROWN INTO A WAR ZONE

Yet there came a day when it was our family, the Huch family, that needed a miracle from God. First we needed a miracle for our baby grandson, Lion. I can't express our dismay when, a year later, Tiz received an equally devastating diagnosis.

Where do you go when you are suddenly thrown into a war zone? Tiz and I went back and stood upon the same rock-solid foundations of spiritual warfare, diligent prayer, and unwavering faith in God's Word. The same way we have faced and overcome every challenge, large or small, is how we faced and overcame these new levels of challenges. We have never faced greater attacks on our family, but we have also never seen greater outpourings of God's grace and miracles!

In the Hebrew language, there is no word for coincidence. That means it is no coincidence you are reading this book right now in this season of your life. It is by the leading of the Lord Himself. I hope you have a foundation of faith already established in your life. I hope you pray for Israel and bless Israel at every opportunity. I don't know where your level of faith is right now, but I want you to walk with us and let your faith grow afresh and strong as you witness what God has done for Tiz, for Lion, and for our whole family.

BACK TO OUR FOUNDATIONS

Prayer and faith are foundations on which you build to see your miracle. Think about the last time God answered your own prayer. God is good! From the day that Tiz and I met as brand-new converts, we both have been serious people of prayer. Over the course of time, we've spent hours on our knees in prayer, asking God to pour out His Spirit upon us and through us. In fact, seeing Tiz's passion for the Lord and her commitment to prayer was one of the most important things that drew me to her. Our marriage, our family, and our ministry are living testaments to the miraculous power of prayer.

With a heart of passion and commitment, Tiz stood by my side and prayed with me through our journeys and challenges over the past four decades. Now it was my turn to stand beside her. Our children stood with us too. We refused to limit God. Together, we stood fully in active faith and prayer as a family, and we believed God would do His miracles, His way, and in His time!

Over our lifetime we have stood in faith and experienced thousands of miracles for ourselves and others in every area of life. As Romans 4:21 says, we live our lives "fully persuaded that God had power to do what he had promised" (NIV). No matter what the challenges, big or small, we stand firm on the foundations of our faith in God, His Word, authority, dominion, and power.

Luke 1:37 says, "For with God nothing will be impossible." Nothing is too big for God! Not cancer. Not leukemia. Not a thing you may be facing right now.

Mark 16:18 gives us the authority to lay hands on the sick and see them recover. In Matthew 16:19, Jesus released to His church incredible authority and power to fight against the kingdom of darkness and establish God's kingdom on earth. He empowers us all with these words, "I will give you the keys of the kingdom of heaven, and whatever you bind on earth will be bound in heaven, and whatever you loose on earth will be loosed in heaven."

The Bible also says, "I can do all things through Christ who strengthens me" (Phil. 4:13). God Almighty has given His children authority and power to walk in and establish His dominion not only in the world but in our health, families, finances, and every other realm of our lives. Through our prayers and faith, we can drive back the forces of darkness and release the power of God's promises. Some might think this sounds presumptuous or overpromising.

I believe if it is in the Bible, it is absolutely true, trustworthy, and literal. If God said it, He meant it, and we can base our lives on it. One of Tiz's favorite declaration scriptures is Isaiah 55:11:

> So shall My word be that goes forth from My mouth; it shall not return to Me void, but it shall accomplish what I please, and it shall prosper in the thing for which I sent it.

We all know that every person has an appointed time to die. Only the Lord knows those dates for each one of us. There have been times when we prayed and believed in faith for people and have not seen healing. There are many unanswered questions we all have on this side of eternity. I certainly don't claim to have all the answers or miracle formulas by any means. Despite this, I still absolutely believe in God's promises for healing. Our faith is not based on circumstances, outcomes, or results. Ecclesiastes 3:11 states, "He has made everything beautiful in its time." I had the deep peace and confidence that, whether my appointed time to be with the Lord was now or later, I would be with Him throughout eternity. You can have that same peace and confidence as well. Our faith is based on God, His Word, and His power. Our testimonies are to tell what has happened for us and to bring hope to others and glory to God. In the uncertainty of cancer diagnoses, we clung to this scripture and saw it come to pass both for Lion and Tiz:

> I shall not die, but live, and declare the works of the LORD.
>
> —PSALM 118:17

FAITH IS ACTIVE AND AGGRESSIVE

In the natural realm, we faced diagnoses, statistics, and reports that were daunting, to say the least. We did absolutely everything we could in the way of medical treatments and followed the directions of our incredible doctors, whom we thank God for. Above and beyond that, we chose to believe and stand on the life-changing power of our God. As Tiz says, God put His *super* to our natural!

Faith is not passive. Faith is active and aggressive. For our entire married life, Tiz and I have aggressively pressed into the promises of God in every sphere of our life and ministry, defeating and overcoming obstacles through the power of God. We are both determined and tenacious to fight for God's best and not settle for what life, the world, or the enemy throws in front of us.

I will talk about Matthew 11:12 quite a bit in the last few chapters of this book. But I want you to know that God's Word is true and "the kingdom of God suffers violence, and the violent take it by force." There was no way I was going to allow these attacks to take the lives of Lion or Tiz. Everything within me would fight violently, aggressively, and consistently against this attack upon my family. I rose up with righteous indignation that the enemy would dare to come against us on these levels.

I come from the streets and grew up a street fighter and boxer. No way was I going to back down and passively let this happen. Not on my watch! We counterattacked cancer day by day in the authority, dominion, and power of the Lord! We put our spiritual foot down and boldly declared, "Nothing but the will of God and His promises will rule and reign in the bodies of Tiz and Lion! The name of our God is above even the name of cancer and leukemia!"

I deliberately spoke out and looked for the hand of God moving. When we would go to the hospital to see Luke, Jen, and Lion, I would tell my family, "We are going to look for and see two significant miracles or breakthroughs today." One day while I was driving up through the hospital's packed high-level parking lot, a parking spot opened up closer to the floor Lion was on. I declared, "Praise God! Confirmation that we are one level closer to Lion going home!"

We don't base our lives on seeing signs, but we sure will take any little signs or confirmations the Lord wants to throw our way. As we were leaving the oncology floor the day of Lion's diagnosis, we were all feeling wiped out and spent. We kept encouraging Luke and Jen and each other with healing scriptures and affirmations such as, "God's got this!" We were waiting at the elevator door and saw a sports magazine on a small table with a cover that read, "You Got This!" Choosing to stay in a positive faith mindset and attitude is critical when entering into God's miracles. We did all we could to look for and expect the Lord to move!

WE WIN

Our hopes, dreams, and prayers were not in vain and have come to pass. Lion and Tiz are both cancer-free, whole, and healthy! Our family is experiencing life together more than ever.

Without a doubt, we saw miracles that were absolutely God's hand of supernatural healing. Our family's healing victories were great encouragements to our medical teams, who work so endlessly hard in tough, challenging circumstances, often not seeing the victories that we have seen. Our doctors were astounded by the incredible results of both Tiz and Lion and admitted, "We did our best, and God did the rest."

When Luke and Jen were finally able to take Lion home from living at the hospital for six months, the doctors, nurses, and specialist gave them a little send-off party of celebration. They all said, "This is such a happy day for all of us. We needed to see a win."

THE POWER OF THE TESTIMONY

Our testimony of hope and healing impacted the lives of those surrounding us. A dear lady told us recently how much watching our TV show has encouraged her in her own battle against cancer. As much as she loved hearing the victory reports of our progress, she said she really loved hearing and seeing how we walked out our faith in our daily lives through the healing journey. She said that although we all love and hope for instant miracles and quick resolutions to our challenges, our reality isn't always that way. She emphasized her appreciation of the endurance of faith, positive attitudes, and victory we exemplified as we journeyed through it all. She stressed that we need to learn how to endure life's challenges while we are contending for God's miracles.

Tiz refers to this as the "in the meantime" process. The time between the attack and the victory is the "in the meantime" process where we walk out our faith. It's here that we see the Lord help, equip, and transform our circumstances through His miracles by the moment.

Our purpose in writing this book is to bring hope, example, and direction that is desperately needed in the world right now. Our stories are more than just victory stories of what the Lord has done for us. They are a guide on how we fought and overcame these huge challenges.

Miracles are real and for everyone. There is God's part and there is our part to bring them to pass. Our victories came in the forms of some incredible, huge miracles and in hundreds of smaller, yet significant miracles, all working together to bring us to these victorious outcomes. Let this be an encouragement to you. This process worked for us, and it can work for you also. What God has done for us, He can do for you!

OUR TOP PRIORITY

Our top priority in our walk of faith is being a blessing to Israel. We don't just teach and preach the biblical commandment to be a blessing to Israel, we live it out in the reality of our lives each and every day. Every morning in our prayers we ask the Lord what He is doing in the world today and how He wants us to be a part of it. Judaism teaches that, as God's people, we have the privilege to partner with the Lord to *tikkun olam*, which is to repair the broken world.[2]

Most people spend their prayer time asking God to bless them, but it is more important to ask God how we can *be* a blessing to Him, His people, and the world. We genuinely live our daily lives in this mindset and momentum.

During the battles we faced with cancer and the immense needs in our own family, it would have seemed only natural to reduce our focus on outreaches and the needs of others in the world. However, our family and ministry staff made the decision not to back off. We determined to press forward in even greater commitments to be a blessing to Israel.

We take God seriously when He says, "I will bless those who bless [Israel]" (Gen. 12:3). Our faith in the spiritual realm always ties in with our commitments to act in the natural realm. We needed God to bless us, answer our prayers, and release miracles in our family. So we chose to *be* a blessing to the people and nation of Israel, *be* an answer to their prayers, and *be* part of God's releasing miracles into their lives and nation.

As we continued our active commitment to *tikkun olam*, or repairing the broken world, God Almighty actively repaired our own broken world and bodies.

As believers we know the Bible tells us that we will reap what we sow (Gal. 6:7). What we cause to happen for others, God will cause to happen for us. In Judaism, our acts of kindness are referred to as our *zehut*, or merits. We are taught that as a regular part of our prayers and petitions, we are given the honor by the Lord to call in our *zehut*—merits, deeds, or seeds sown for His work.[3]

Our God is a just and righteous God who honors and rewards His people. Let me emphasize that we absolutely do not earn God's miracles by our works. We receive His miraculous salvation, help, and miracles by His love, grace, and mercy. However, the Bible tells us over and over, "As we sow, we shall also reap." Let me encourage you to follow this biblical pattern and our example of *tikkun olam* in your own life. Giving is a boomerang that always returns and multiplies back into our own lives.

FOUNDATION OF POSITIVE
THOUGHTS, WORDS, AND ACTIONS

Winning the battle of cancer in the spiritual realm begins with winning the battle in our minds. Tiz and I will teach more on the weapons of our warfare throughout the book, but for now let me focus on Ephesians 6:17, putting on the helmet of our salvation.

> And take the helmet of salvation, and the sword of the Spirit, which is the word of God; praying always with all prayer and supplication in the Spirit, being watchful to this end with all perseverance and supplication for all the saints.
>
> —EPHESIANS 6:17–18

I cannot emphasize enough how essential our helmet is to winning our battles! Most of our battles begin in our minds. That is why it is so important to protect our minds with the helmet of salvation. God wants you to learn how to take every thought captive and bring it to the obedience of Christ.

> For the weapons of our warfare *are* not carnal but mighty in God for pulling down strongholds, casting down arguments and every high thing that exalts itself against the knowledge of God, bringing every thought into captivity to the obedience of Christ.
>
> —2 CORINTHIANS 10:4–5

The enemy will always try to get you to think and worry about the negative things in your life. But God tells you in His Word to think about and meditate only on those things that are pure, true, noble, just, lovely, and praiseworthy. (See Philippians 4:8).

You probably fight this battle every day—negative thoughts challenging positive thoughts. To win this battle, you need to renew your mind to the Word of God.

And do not be conformed to this world, but be transformed by the renewing of your mind, that you may prove what *is* that good and acceptable and perfect will of God.

—ROMANS 12:2

THE CHALLENGE WILL BACK DOWN FROM YOU

God wants us to live a transformed life, but we have to learn to align our thoughts, words, and actions with the Bible. The result? *Instead of you fearfully backing down from the challenge, the challenge will back down from you!*

Tiz loves to tell people, "Change your thinking, and you will change your life!"

Each day when you pray, make it a point to cover your mind with the helmet of salvation. Receive the mind of Christ with all wisdom, knowledge, faith, and understanding. As you change the way you think, you will see your life change for the better every day. See your life, health, finances, and circumstances through the eyes of God, and watch His blessings and miracles begin to flow!

ALL THINGS WORK FOR YOUR GOOD

Next to John 3:16, our favorite scripture in the Bible is Romans 8:28: "We know that all things work together for good to those who love God, to those who are the called according to His purpose."

Tiz and I know, from more than forty-five years of serving God together, that the Lord will take what the enemy has meant for evil and use it for our good. No matter what obstacle or attack we're facing, we must continue to walk by faith, keep our attitude positive, and fulfill God's purpose. God will always bring unexpected blessings and miracle breakthroughs. We just need to keep our eyes on Him and not the circumstances. Even when circumstances are difficult or unresolved for periods of time, we can always find peace and victory in knowing that God will cause *all* things to work together for good!

TAKE UP YOUR SHIELD OF FAITH

Ephesians 6:16 tells us, "Above all, taking the shield of faith with which you will be able to quench all the fiery darts of the wicked one."

You'll discover that the shield of faith not only protects you personally, but when you join with like-minded believers, it will protect families, neighborhoods, cities, and even nations!

Romans 10:17 says that faith comes by hearing God's Word. When you saturate yourself with God's Word, your faith will be able to quench every fiery dart of the enemy or the world.

No matter what you are facing in your life, determine to stay in a mindset of positive faith in the Lord and His promises. Give Him all praise because we know that all things work together for our good. Thank Him for His protection against all the fiery darts of the enemy. Receive His strengthening in your faith through all the promises in the Word of God, and expect the best because our God is a miracle-working God, and nothing is impossible for Him.

When Tiz and I and our family needed giant miracles, we stood on the giant foundations and promises in the Word of God. We focused not on our giant problems but on His giant promises. We sought not just the giant miracles but the giant miracle worker! We will teach you how to do the same in your own needs and lives. Our God, who delivered us and brought us through, can do the same for you!

CHAPTER 3

FAITH AT A WHOLE NEW LEVEL

TIZ HUCH

L ARRY AND I have always been determined to trust God and believe His promises. We have overcome many challenges over our years together as man and wife and as a ministry team. However, I will admit it, this C diagnosis was a whole new level of giant to overcome.

On the day of our doctor visit, when we finally had a moment alone, our words of faith tumbled out immediately: "Nothing is too hard for our God!" Yet inwardly I knew that this time it was literally life or death. I knew deep down that we needed to grasp some new level of faith.

On our drive home from the oncologist, we discussed everything the doctor said, realizing that he presented few options and that the diagnosis required immediate action.

Whether you have symptoms of a cold, COVID-19, or cancer, the name of Jesus Christ the Lord is higher and more authoritative than any other name. The Lord is our Shepherd and chief physician. His analysis and His Word trump any doctor report. We knew that.

"He certainly won't let us down now," Larry said.

"He didn't bring us this far to leave us," I said, agreeing.

For years we prayed for the sick and saw God heal them, either instantly or through a process. In my heart I could hear each of us declaring from the podium, "Whose report will we believe? We will believe the report of the Lord!" Always!

NO CONFLICT BETWEEN MEDICAL AND SPIRITUAL REALMS

We do not believe that there should be a conflict between the medical realm and the spiritual realm. We have believed and prayed for thousands of people over the years, including ourselves and our own family. Sometimes we see instantaneous miraculous results. We sure love that! Sometimes we don't see those results right away. The Bible says that Jesus did so many great miracles that they couldn't even fit it all into one book. Many were instantaneous, colossal miracles. When we read the Gospels, we see numerous accounts of people raised from the dead, blind eyes opened, bondages broken, and demon-possessed people freed. No doubt, Jesus performed supernatural, genuine miracles.

The Gospels also record that at other times the sickness was arrested and the healing process began. A blind man was brought to Jesus. Jesus spit into his eyes! Then He laid hands on the blind man and asked him, "Do you see anything?" Let's look at the blind man's answer in this account:

> And he looked up and said, "I see men like trees, walking." Then He put His hands on his eyes again and made him look up. And he was restored and saw everyone clearly.
> —MARK 8:24–25

The blind man saw a little bit at first, but he didn't see completely right away. What did Jesus do? He put his hands on the blind man's eyes one more time. The healing of the blind man was a true miracle, but this time it didn't happen immediately. If you are in a process of healing or a process of full restoration, continue on in your faith. You will obtain the victory!

If you are praying for someone else who needs a miracle in his or her life, keep praying. If they are open to it, lay your hands on them as Jesus laid His hands on the blind man.

THE ROAD TO HEALING

In Mark 16:18, Jesus said that His followers will lay hands on the sick and they will recover. Sometimes they recover immediately. Sometimes healing materializes over a progression of time and faith.

Our approach, through years of walking in faith, is to do everything we can to see healing and miracles, big or small. The end goal on our road to healing is to see our bodies healed, and we use every means possible—spiritual, natural, and medical. We thank God for the medical teams, machines, medicines, and treatments, and in my own healing journey we did all that was possible to get the best medical treatment available. Larry and I were determined to walk, talk, and live in faith and declare God's promises over our lives and over my body every day—every time we thought about my need for healing.

LIVING BY FAITH IN THE NATURAL REALM

While we stand in faith in the supernatural, we do not live in denial of what is going on in the natural realm. It is not wise to bury our heads in the sand and deny realities in the natural realm.

When the oncologist walked in with my test results in his hands and said, "Your CT scan and ultrasound reveal that you have aggressive, stage 3 ovarian cancer," we did not jump up and deny the test results. However, we definitely denied cancer's right to rule and reign in my body or in Lion's body!

Walking in faith doesn't mean we completely ignore the natural circumstances. Each Christian has to deal with the realities they are facing, whether in their health, family, finances, relationships, or work. We see those realities, but we deny their right to rule and reign in our lives. We live in a real world with real circumstances.

I hope this viewpoint on seeing our natural realities is a comfort to you. Faith doesn't mean we ignore issues or turn a blind eye to them. Faith certainly doesn't mean we don't tell or ask other believers to pray for us!

Faith means that when we confront challenges or issues, we face them head-on and rise up above them with every means possible.

LOVED CONQUERORS

The Bible says we are "more than conquerors." If there was nothing to conquer, then Paul would not have told us this. This verse plainly shows us that God will put His *super* into our *natural*. Praise God for His *super*natural!

It's important to grasp that we are conquerors—and that biblical faith and medical technology and treatments are not in conflict or opposition to each other.

Why are we more than conquerors? Is it because we are faith giants? No. We are more than conquerors because we are loved by a mighty, miracle-working God!

> Yet in all these things we are more than conquerors through Him who loved us. For I am persuaded that neither death nor life, nor angels nor principalities nor powers, nor things present nor things to come, nor height nor depth, nor any other created thing, shall be able to separate us from the love of God which is in Christ Jesus our Lord.
>
> —ROMANS 8:37–39

You see, it's the love of God that makes us conquerors. It's the love of God that's kept Larry and me strong for more than four decades of marriage and ministry. First John 4:19 says, "We love Him because He first loved us." Oh, the love of God! And *we* conquer because *Jesus* conquers. The love of God constrains us to pour out our lives to help people break strongholds and destructive patterns. As a popular car insurance commercial says, we know a few things 'cause we've seen a few things. That's the truth!

My friend, Larry and I want you to succeed and be blessed in every area of your life. That's why we are sharing our life experience in this book. We want you to know that you are not alone in the struggles of life. We want you to have hope and understand that we've been there too, and guess what? *You* are more than a conqueror. And no matter what your circumstance is telling you, we can assure you right now that you are a loved conqueror, and Jesus wins!

CHAPTER 4

A FIERCE BATTLE FOR LION'S LIFE

TIZ HUCH

W E WILL NEVER forget the moment when Luke and Jen surprised us and told us they were pregnant. Our whole family literally screamed, jumped up and down, and cried in ecstatic joy. Yes, I jumped up and down, and yes, Larry cried!

Our entire family was at the hospital when our long-awaited baby Lion was born, and we made so much noise over his arrival that the nurses came out and told us to keep it down! We all adored him and couldn't get enough of him. We have been and are the same way about our other three grandkids, our "sugars." Our children, their spouses, and our sugars are the light and joy of our lives. Each one of them has a unique personality, special giftings, and amazing destinies. We all agreed there was a special spark within Lion. He was always smiling, laughing, and taking in everything, even as a tiny baby. We knew Lion had a great destiny ahead of him.

LION'S DIAGNOSIS

Scroll forward seven months. After Lion received his routine vaccines, he immediately began to run a fever and cry inconsolably. This persisted through the days ahead. Luke and Jen went back to the doctor to figure out what was going on. After multiple emergency room trips, Lion was finally admitted to the children's hospital, where they began a series of intensive tests to find the source of the symptoms. Luke and Jen stayed with Lion night and day, never leaving his side.

After Lion underwent several weeks of testing, the director of children's oncology came to Lion's hospital room to tell Luke and Jen the results. Luke was holding baby Lion as he and Jen heard the heartbreaking news no parents ever want to hear: their baby had a rare form of leukemia. A few moments later, our entire family was in the room. Luke and Jen were still sobbing as they shared the devastating news with us.

The doctor explained that there is no cure and only a 47 percent survival rate for this kind of childhood cancer. The bone marrow test showed that nearly 90 percent of Lion's spinal fluid was filled with cancer cells. Because Lion was only seven months old, his chance of survival dropped sharply due to the increased chances of infection, complications, an undeveloped immune system and organs, and increased risks being even harder to survive at his age.

After the knockout punch of the diagnosis and hours of signing consent forms, Luke, Jen, and Lion were led to the hospital's fifth floor. At the time, they didn't realize it was a cancer floor for kids.

The doctor said, "You guys will live here on the oncology floor while Lion starts chemotherapy today, and tomorrow we will put a central line in his chest that will be connected to his heart. There will be two cords hanging out of his chest until his two-year chemotherapy treatment plan is over."

That central line ended up hanging well below his diaper line because they aren't made for infants, which indicates how rare this situation really was. Lion immediately underwent intense chemotherapy treatment and would receive chemo every day, several times a day, for the next two years. They lived in that small hospital room for fifty straight days and a combined total of over six months while Lion received chemotherapy, treatments, tests, and care.

THE DAY LIFE CHANGED

We were all stunned. Just seven months prior, our family was all together in a hospital room rejoicing over him. Now we were together again in a hospital room, but we were all in anguish over baby Lion's intense pain and devastating diagnosis.

As the doctor unveiled the prognosis and procedures ahead, the heaviness in the room became nearly unbearable. Jen hunched over and sobbed on Luke's shoulder. Luke cradled baby Lion closely, crying into his baby blanket. Dear little Lion cried out again and again because of the pain in his tiny body. We all squeezed in tight together to hug and support Luke and Jen as they tried to absorb so much so fast.

Life changed that day. There were statistics and a litany of medical information to take in, schedules to figure out, questions to be asked, answers to be found, prayers to be prayed, emotions to be processed—and work to be done.

As the doctors, specialists, nurses, and hospital chaplain wrapped things up for the time being that day, we could see that the head doctor wanted to speak to us.

OUR DOCTOR WANTED TO PRAY

The head doctor said, "I can see that you and your family are all strong believers. I'm assuming that you are going to have a prayer together now. Would it be all right if we stayed and were a part of your prayers? We all need God's help and miracles too."

"Of course, it would be an honor," we said.

So we all held hands, and Larry led us in a powerful prayer for Lion's peace, supernatural healing, and miracles. We prayed for Luke, Jen, our family, and for the hospital team to have God's equipping, vision, peace, and anointing to do what He had called them to. Then the hospital team left us alone and gave us some space as a family to talk together.

Each one of us was completely drained. I will be honest. We struggled in the natural realm to get any kind of handle on this.

FAITH IS NOT DENYING THE CIRCUMSTANCES—IT'S RISING ABOVE THEM

Although we were still reeling from the news, we felt better after the prayer and agreed that God had everything in His hands. In fact, "God's got this" became our family motto.

However, in the natural Lion was still crying in pain, and Luke and Jen still had a long journey ahead of them. As much as we believed God would turn this around, when we opened our eyes from prayer, in the natural we couldn't see that anything had changed with Lion yet. Although we were standing on God's promises in the spiritual realm, we still had to walk out the steps in the natural realm.

Faith for a miracle doesn't mean we are denying what is going on in the physical realm. We weren't denying the symptoms and medical reports given, but we absolutely denied the cancer's right to rule and reign in Lion's body. Lion's life belonged to God, not to a medical diagnosis or statistic. His future would be defined by God, not by the pain he was experiencing the day we prayed. Our family's faith would remain defined by the power of God's promises, not by the gravity of leukemia.

LIFE'S REALITIES HAVE TO BE DEALT WITH

Our faith was in place, but life kept moving. Luke and Jen and each of us had to get up, pitch in, and do what needed to be done. Luke and Jen gathered up baby Lion and all their things and moved into their new "home" for the next six months—Lion's hospital room on the children's oncology floor. Working with the nurses, they immediately got Lion ready to have a central line placed into his heart the following day. Meanwhile, his chemo and other infusions would begin within the next few hours.

Time was precious, so they rushed Lion off for another spinal tap, blood work, and more tests. They signed piles of paperwork and began the learning process so Lion's treatments could start right away. There was not much time for grieving and comforting each other. Lion's medical journey had begun, and we all had to pull ourselves together and rise to the challenges.

The hospital team took over to help Luke, Jen, and Lion make the move. Larry and I, Anna and her husband, Brandin, and Katie all took off work to gather the things Luke and Jen needed for their daily life and took them back to the hospital room.

We've always known that when someone experiences a traumatic event, one of the greatest ways to show support and love is to take some of the load off their to-do lists. Anna, Katie, and Brandin went to Luke and Jen's house to do their laundry and get them all clean clothes, diapers for Lion, and other essentials they needed.

Larry and I headed to the store to buy them food, necessities, and baby supplies for their new residence, the hospital room. As Larry and I pulled out of the hospital parking lot and onto the highway, we were both uttering declarations of faith to each other and to God.

Suddenly the dam burst, and I sobbed and shook uncontrollably. Larry wept too, but he had to hold himself together to drive. He wiped his red eyes, handed me a tissue, and patted me on the back. He tried to reassure me that this was going to turn around and Lion would be fine. We both believed that, but we were brokenhearted and reeling from the weight of it all. We cried the entire twenty-minute drive to the store. As we parked, we wiped our eyes, blew our noses, pulled ourselves together, and walked into the store.

I struggle right now as I write these memories.

I'll never forget how strange it felt as we walked into the store carrying this horrific trauma. This was the last place in the world we wanted to be. We felt out of touch with normal life and in a fog. The store was busy and loud as people went about their normal shopping, browsing, chatting, laughing, arguing, and everyday living. Larry and I stood there with heavy hearts and watched the world go on as if nothing were abnormal. How does one buy toothpaste, shampoo, baby diapers, formula, and baby wipes when your world has just turned upside down?

Larry and I chose a few little toys that might amuse Lion but could easily be wiped down and sanitized. Next to us was a young, frustrated mom with her toddler in a shopping cart. The child was crying and screaming for a toy he wanted. The moment made me think of how much we all take normal, everyday life for granted. I wondered when we would have the opportunity to push Lion through the toy aisle. Here we were, feeling so overwhelmed and emotionally fragile, just trying to choose a little toy while Luke, Jen, and baby Lion were in the hospital in a fight for his life. It seemed so petty to be in a store shopping for baby toys and toothpaste. Yet normal life goes on, even in the midst of devastation.

How strange to be surrounded by hundreds of people yet feel all alone.

A trainload of thoughts went through my mind: "Does anyone even know or care? Is anyone able to help me? Even if everyone around us knew what we were dealing with, would anyone really understand or care? And even if they did care, could anyone do anything to help us through or change Lion's situation?"

LION'S LIFE ON THE FIFTH FLOOR

Lion's tiny hospital room on the fifth floor had only a crib and a small recliner squeezed between all kinds of medical machines and equipment. There was a small bathroom, no kitchen facilities, and no beds for Mommy and Daddy to sleep in. As it turned out, Jen would sleep (or try to sleep in between the twenty-minute nurse checkups, meds, diaper changes, and so on) wrapped around Lion in the hospital crib, dodging all the cords and IV lines he was connected to. Luke would try to dose off in the stiff recliner with his head propped up on a pillow.

Please understand, we were all incredibly thankful for the outstanding teams of doctors and nurses. The hospital is top shelf, and I don't want to appear ungrateful or complaining. I'm just trying to create an accurate picture of how drastically our world changed.

Abruptly, our seven-month-old grandbaby left his world of stroller rides through the park, snuggling with Mommy and Daddy as he lay between them in bed, and rolling around and playing on the floor. Larry and I keenly felt the absence of Lion's visits to our home for family dinners. Baby Lion endured being plugged into IVs and monitors 24/7 while living in the hospital. Luke and Jen squeezed their lives, jobs, and family time into a tiny hospital room. They lived like this in the hospital for a total of six months over the course of two years during which Lion received chemo for almost eight hundred days straight. In the blink of an eye, the joy and laughter turned into sorrow and anguish.

ALL ALONE IN A CROWDED ROOM

Perhaps you've experienced feeling all alone in a crowded room. It's strange how we can be surrounded by people yet feel isolated or trapped, especially if we are in a personal crisis that no one around us knows about.

Seeing everyone around you just carrying on with their normal, everyday lives can create feelings of isolation and loneliness. It feels like a movie scene where the whole world is carrying on as normal while you are completely frozen in time.

If you are reading this book and reaching out for someone to care, please know that God sees you and cares about you. God may use a person to come and talk to you, or He may draw you into a time of private prayer with just the two of you exchanging your cares for His plans. Trust Him. Believe Him. He is right there with you, even now.

PRAYING GOD'S PROMISES

In tears, our family instinctively started to pray together. We groped in the darkness of this disease and found God's promises were still there. Together we drew from the deep deposits of God's Word, led by His wonderful Spirit within our souls. We could tangibly feel ourselves reaching up out of the natural realm of reports and statistics as we spoke positive words of faith.

There are hundreds of promises in Scripture declaring hope, healing, and miracles. A few of the key scriptures we personalized and declared are:

- You are the God that healeth me (Exod. 15:26).

- You will take sickness away from the midst of me, and the number of my days You will fulfill (Exod. 23:25–26).

- You sent Your Word and healed me and delivered me from my destructions (Ps. 107:20).

- I shall not die, but live, and declare Your works (Ps. 118:17).

- You cause breath to enter into me, and I shall live. And You put Your Spirit in me, and I shall live (Ezek. 37:5, 14).

MIRACLES BY THE MOMENT

Sometimes a miracle comes in the form of one enormous, instantaneous phenomenon. More often, though, a miracle comes to us in the form of many smaller miracles that add up to one giant miracle.

Yes, the doctors declared Lion cancer-free on day fifty of his chemo treatment. This was an enormous breakthrough. The story didn't end there, though. Over the remainder of his two-year treatment, many ensuing challenges were all met with miracles—big, small, and everything in between!

As much as the Lord astounded us with Lion's miracle, we also saw him sustain Luke and Jen with daily faith, courage, strength, direction, wisdom, endurance, love, peace, and joy that transcended their circumstances. Also, Lion emerged out of nearly eight hundred days of chemo with no permanent damage to his organs or mental or physical functions. In fact, he has above-average growth and is gifted intellectually and musically, proving that God can do "exceedingly abundantly above all that we ask or think" (Eph. 3:20).

Of course, we are all cheering for that instant miracle, but our family has grown to thank God for the continual flow of miracles by the moment!

ALL THINGS WORK TOGETHER FOR GOOD

As I mentioned previously, our family motto became "God's got this!" We based our prayers and declarations around one of our main life verses: Romans 8:28.

We prayed: "Lord, though we may not be able to understand all that is going on, we choose to trust You, and we give this all to You. We know that no matter what this looks like, what this evolves into, or how it plays out, we stand firm on Your promise that all things work together for the good of those who love You and are called according to Your purposes. We trust You, Your Word, and Your promises. We *know* that You will bring good out of this. We *know* You will weave a beautiful tapestry out of all this chaos. We raise our voices and hearts right now to give You glory, praise, and honor. Amen."

I mentioned earlier that Larry and I have lived by Romans 8:28 our entire lives. We taught our children this verse too, and now as adults they've chosen to live by it as well. There have been many times when circumstances looked grim and scary, but God never failed to turn things around. He brought something good and better out of it all!

Sometimes when we are under attack, we can barely squeak out a little peep of a prayer, raise even a little finger in praise, or murmur a promise from God's Word. But when we choose to trust Him and believe His promises, His Spirit and power invade us. God equips us with His Word and enables us to rise above, cope with, and conquer whatever is coming against us.

"Greater is he that is in you, than he that is in the world"

(1 John 4:4, KJV). My version of this verse is, "Greater is He who is within me than he who is chasing me or attacking me."

We can't always understand the hows, whys, or wherefores, but we can always count on the promises of our God. Our God is good, loving, and all-powerful. Choose to trust Him!

There is so much more to tell about this journey, and we will share the details of Lion's miracle later in this book. As Larry said before, this story gets better. We did everything possible medically and in the natural realm. And then we saw God put His *super* to our *natural*!

However, our goal is not just to share our story but to build your faith for the miracle you need in your life. How do you do that? First you must get to know the miracle worker Himself.

CHAPTER 5

DO NOT SEEK THE MIRACLE— SEEK THE MIRACLE WORKER

Tiz Huch

D O YOU KNOW there are more than eight thousand promises in the Bible? That's a lot of promises! But more important than knowing or reciting those eight thousand promises is knowing the promise giver Himself. When we know God—really *know* Him—it is easy to believe that He has only the very best in His heart for us.

Can God work a miracle in your life? Of course He can. But only an immature child looks to a parent for what he or she can "get" out of that relationship. Maturing sons and daughters want to know their parent and spend time with them.

LOOK TO GOD

The first step to experiencing God's miracles is to spend time with Him and actually *know* Him. To know His names (and their meanings) and His promises is to trust Him. Take the time in your daily life to develop a relationship with God. This is the most important foundation for living a life of miracles. The foremost priority of the believer is to look to our God. We must look to Him through Scripture and the leading of the Holy Spirit so we can see how caring and fabulous He is! This concept is summed up by the Hebrew word *avot*, which means "the first" and refers to the most important and foundational things in our lives.

Larry taught earlier that *avot* (or *avos*, the plural form) refers to the beginnings of a thing, and those beginnings are the all-important foundation that must be continued and built upon. The way something begins determines how it will ultimately finish. Again, we can look at this like the top button on a button-down shirt—if you don't get the top one buttoned right, none of the other buttons will line up. But when you match the top button to the correct buttonhole, everything else lines up perfectly and easily. Our relationship with God is our top priority, our "top button."

So how do we get to know God? As I said, the way a thing begins determines the way it progresses and turns out. So every morning, before you dive into all your to-do lists or responsibilities, dive into His presence. As you breathe your first breaths of the morning, stop and breathe in God's breath of life. Focus on Jesus and connect yourself to His Word, His love, and His peace.

Larry and I have personally practiced this, in good times and tough times, and taught this to others for more than forty-five years. Knowing God—having an intimate relationship with Him—is the absolute most important key to living consistently in His presence.

You see, experiencing miracles by the moment is the outflow of a deep, consistent pursuit of God. I'm not talking about a theory; I'm talking about my actual experience of knowing God. When we make knowing Him the *avot*, the top button, of our days and lives, everything else lines up accordingly. Let's not wait until we need a miracle to become acquainted with the miracle worker!

My top priority in seeking my miracle healing of cancer was to seek the Lord Himself. To intimately know Him, His nature, and His love has always been my goal. I want to commune with God. I had so much to do and deal with during this time, but I knew that above all my future depended on saturating my heart, mind, soul, and body with the Spirit of the living God. The most important thing on my long to-do list was to spend time in His presence.

The second–most important thing was to saturate myself with His promises on healing. I needed to elevate my spirit, mind, and emotions into a high level of confidence that I was not going to die from this cancer. No! I was going to be healed by God! I live by faith in God's promises, but the severity of this life-threatening disease required an entirely new level of faith and spiritual warfare.

Later in this book you will see my daily routine of quoting Scripture. For now, you may want to check out the appendix to see 101 verses on healing you can declare right now on a daily basis. The sense of peace, normalcy, and joy that overrode my circumstances was tangible. In fact, so many people commented that they were astounded by how positive Larry and I were as we told our church family about what was happening and encouraged them to believe everything would turn out great.

In your own life, no matter what you're facing, dedicate time to spend in the presence of God, worshipping and glorifying Him. Let His presence envelop and elevate you into His reality. Declare the promises from the Word of God. Rather than dwelling on and magnifying the problems, dwell on and magnify His promises. Think and talk about His love, goodness, and limitless power to change your life and circumstances. Now let me explain how to do this.

YĀDAʿ—TO KNOW AND TRUST HIM

The Hebrew word know (yāḍaʿ), like our word know in English, can have various meanings. It can indicate mental knowledge in that a person understands or has knowledge of something. But the concept of knowing something or someone takes on a specialized meaning in the Hebrew language when it has to do with relationship—especially a relationship made through covenant.

In the Bible, the Hebrew word yāḍaʿ can mean to acknowledge the terms of a covenant one has entered into, loyalty, or keeping your word.[1] Let's look at the usage of the word *know* in Genesis 18:19 (emphasis added):

> For I *know* him, that he will command his children and his household after him, and they shall keep the way of the LORD, to do justice and judgment; that the LORD may bring upon Abraham that which he hath spoken of him.

It's interesting to note that the word *yāḏaʿ* is often translated as "chosen" in Genesis 18:19. Notice how the verse reads in the New International Version (emphasis added):

> For I have *chosen* him, so that he will direct his children and his household after him to keep the way of the LORD by doing what is right and just, so that the LORD will bring about for Abraham what he has promised him.

The Lord is saying in this verse that He knows Abraham and trusts him to keep his side of the covenant. This implies a depth of confidence and intimacy in the relationship. It is important to understand that God's covenant was not based upon the fact that Abraham was a perfect man. Abraham wasn't perfect. So perfection did not make Abraham worthy of God's covenant. The Scriptures are very open about Abraham's and Sarah's human weaknesses. But God and Abraham had an interactive and intimate relationship that involved *yāḏaʿ*—knowing and trusting each other.

Think about it. The Lord *knew* He could trust Abraham, and Abraham *knew* he could trust the Lord. Do you know that you can trust the Lord? The basis for trusting someone is to first know him. To know God is to trust Him, and for Him to know us is to trust us. That is what a covenant relationship between the Lord and us looks like. Wow!

Whether the concept of an intimate relationship with the Lord is new to you or you are a seasoned prayer warrior, exciting new adventures with God await us all. Let's make the choice to commit ourselves to knowing God right now. Whether it is an hour or five minutes, dedicate time to Him alone first thing each morning. Make knowing Him the way you begin your day. God is ready, willing, and available to you.

HE KNOWS YOUR NAME

In ancient Hebrew, the concept of knowing is similar to the English understanding of knowing but on a much more personal and intimate level. We may say we know someone but simply mean we know of their existence or have briefly met them. In Hebrew thought, we can know someone only if we have a personal and intimate relationship with them.

Genesis 4:1 says Adam "knew Eve his wife," implying a very intimate union between husband and wife. In Genesis 18:19, the Lord says about Abraham, "I have known him," meaning God had a very close friendship with Abraham. In fact, James 2:23 says, "'Abraham believed God, and it was accounted to him for righteousness.' And he was called the friend of God."

How incredible is it that God would offer you and me the opportunity to actually know Him as a close, personal friend! The more we study the Scriptures, the more we see the longing of God's heart to know each one of us.

If you look up John 10:14, you will see that Jesus calls Himself the Good Shepherd. Jesus said, "I am the good shepherd; and I know My sheep, and am known by My own." Earlier in that same chapter, in verse 3, Jesus said the Good Shepherd calls His own sheep by name!

Have you considered this? Do you realize that Jesus knows your name? Have you ever heard the voice of God? Have you heard Jesus call you by name?

Larry talks often about hearing the voice of God. It is possible to hear God's voice inside your spirit. Consider these words of Jesus:

My sheep hear My voice, and I know them, and they
follow Me. And I give them eternal life, and they shall
never perish; neither shall anyone snatch them out of
My hand.

—JOHN 10:27–28

Jesus makes it so plain to us here that He knows each one of
us. Every person who has believed in Him will have eternal life,
and no one can take that away from us. Praise God! Each person
who has received Jesus as their Savior will be known by Jesus
and hear His voice. What a treasure we have here on earth, to
know the Lord Jesus!

SEEK HIM ABOVE ALL

Second Peter 3:18 tells us to "grow in the grace and knowledge
of our Lord and Savior Jesus Christ." Are you growing in your
knowledge of the Lord? Do you long to know Him as your closest
friend?

Our Lord Jesus desires to have a genuine, living, fresh,
evolving, and intimate relationship with each of us. He has given
us open-door access to Him. What an outrageous opportunity!
However, it is really up to us to discipline ourselves to carve out
the time and make the effort to press in to know Him. I know
how busy and complex our lives are, believe me. I am not saying
this to be harsh or condescending. I am preaching to the choir
(myself) right now. I know that God sees and understands the
mountains of tasks we all have to complete and how stretched we
are to make ends meet and take care of all the issues of our lives.
But the fact still remains that we ultimately miss out on taking
our relationship with Him to new levels when we don't seek Him.
We shortchange ourselves of so much He wants to do within us,
for us, and through us.

Let me give you an example. Not long ago I had a lengthy
conversation with a woman who was very depressed. She had
come to a breaking point after years of dealing with multiple

traumas including a messy divorce, several other failed relation-ships, financial problems, mounting health challenges, and per-sonal inner turmoil. She was at such a low point emotionally that she was physically sick, unable to hold food down, and having increasing thoughts of suicide.

Earlier in her life she had known the Lord, gone to church, and served God. Over the years she had slipped away from Him and was no longer living for Him.

I felt such sadness and compassion for her as she poured out her heart to me. In desperation she asked if I could pray for her to break the strongholds over her mind and life. I told her that of course I would pray for her and that God could set her free and bring change to her life. I then told her how much I cared for her and that I wanted to help her get emotional relief. However, if she genuinely wanted change to take place, it wouldn't come from someone else's prayers. It wouldn't come from *outside* of her. Lasting peace and wholeness would only come from a change *within* her.

You see, I knew that the only way she would rise up out of this deep oppression was to ask the Lord into her heart and allow His Spirit to change her from the inside out. I encouraged her not just to seek the miracle but to seek the miracle worker.

She said, "Yes, I want the Lord back in my heart and life."

I prayed and then led her in a prayer, and the most incredible peace filled not only the room but also her heart, mind, and body. Tears of joy burst from her as the Holy Spirit poured Himself into her, bringing relief and genuine joy. She called me later that night and again the next morning to let me know God had touched her deeply and set her free, and He was already turning her circumstances for the better! In fact, she still updates me on the list of blessings and miracles God has brought into her life and family. Our God is a good God—all the time.

There are a few important points to this story that are relevant to knowing God and His promises.

- She previously knew the Lord.

- She knew a few scriptures.

- She even kept a little Bible in her nightstand.

All of this was good, but they did nothing to help her when she was depressed and suicidal. A little head knowledge of God and His Word or a Bible tucked away will do little to affect us, change us, or give us freedom from our circumstances. The woman's heart, mind, life, and challenges were changed only when she genuinely came to know Him.

CARVE OUT TIME EACH DAY

In an ideal scenario, we would start and end our days with hours of prayer and Bible study. To begin carving out time with the Lord, let's commit to spending at least fifteen to thirty minutes in prayer and devotions each morning. I promise you, it will be time well spent that will change your life for the better.

How do you begin? Pick up your Bible, bow your head, and say, "Lord, I deeply desire to know You as my dearest friend. I want to commit the first part of my day to You right now. Please speak to me."

EIGHT THOUSAND PROMISES TO APPLY TO YOUR LIFE

As I mentioned, God Himself has given us more than eight thousand incredible promises in the Bible. Here are just a few of them:

- divine help

- health

- provision

- peace

- joy

- long life

- blessed family
- blessings on your work

What a list of promises! As you enter into a more intimate relationship with the miracle maker, you will find it easy to lay hold of the promises He has made. No matter what challenges you are facing right now, God has a promise to fit your situation. In fact, before you ever faced the problem in front of you, God already prepared the answer for you.

The most important thing is to commit to making God first in your day. Open your Bible and ask Him to show you one of those eight thousand promises—a special one just for you.

CHAPTER 6

FAITH INFUSIONS FOR THE SOUL
TIZ HUCH

S EVERAL YEARS AGO, before any of the recent health chaos, I had an idea to start a daily devotional blog called "Soul Infusions" or "Faith Infusions." I ran with it for a little while but then didn't find time to continue with it. The word *infusion* is used commonly in the medical world, and it means to inject fluids directly into the bloodstream. Little did I realize back then how much I would need faith infusions for my soul as I received chemo infusions for my body! However, what I want to share with you in this chapter does not just apply to chemo days—it applies to daily life.

Every four weeks I went to the hospital's infusion center, where I would receive an IV in my arm that fed chemo and other drugs into my bloodstream to kill any cancer cells in my body. The process takes several hours. The advancements in cancer treatment over the years have been amazing, and I thank God for them and for the medical professionals in this field. I must say, though, that a chemo infusion is not an afternoon picnic.

MY CHEMO VERSE

The anxiety of the whole chemo process was a huge issue all its own. As much as I believed in my mind and spirit that everything was going to turn out for the good, I still had to walk the journey out in the natural every day and every moment. That's why my motto became "miracles by the moment."

The chemo routine is pretty intense. It's very troubling to know the chemo going into your body will kill off cancer cells. Of course, I wondered, "If it will kill off those cells, what else might it kill off or damage? If it is toxic enough to peel the skin off Lion's little baby feet, what else might it do? If it is making me feel nauseated and sick, how hard is this going to be on my body?" You get the idea.

As I took the chemo infusion, I would quote this scripture with confidence:

> These signs will follow those who believe…if they drink anything deadly, it will by no means hurt them; they will lay hands on the sick, and they will recover.
> —MARK 16:17–18

I determined to take chemo and all medications with faith that they would help my body without deadly side effects.

HOW WE GOT THROUGH

Now that this is all in my rearview mirror, I can say that God really did perform miracles by the moment. But hindsight faith is much easier than foresight faith. When you've made it onto the other side of the chasm, it is much easier to rejoice. But when you're standing in front of that chasm, trying to figure out how you're going to reach the other side, it's hard to breathe. Not only do you have to deal with the physical nausea and achiness, but you also have to deal with the anxiety of the chemo infusion coming up again so quickly.

Let me say that it is not normal for me to talk about the nitty-gritty details of the things I've dealt with. Larry and I have always chosen to live life on the sunny side. Rather than magnify the problems we've faced, we've always magnified the promises

God has given and fulfilled in our lives. Cancer is in our rear-view mirror now, and that's where it's staying!

Our goal is not to tell you all about what we went through. Our goal is to tell you all about how we *got* through!

FAITH INFUSIONS STEP-BY-STEP

If you've walked with someone through cancer, you know there is a heaviness that permeates the cancer treatment centers. People are in various stages of treatment and of facing their new reality. Grieving families gather in hallways or can be heard through thin walls. The waiting rooms are packed with many who are hunched over in physical pain, along with their nervous family members.

Over the months you become familiar with some people, and it's not easy to be surrounded by the visible possibilities of your own future. I'm not trying to sound grim; I'm describing the world of the sick.

Katie, Anna, Brandin, Luke, Jen, Larry, and I entered these corridors deliberately trying to bring encouragement, a smile, and a warm hello to patients while expressing appreciation to the hospital staff.

Each time I entered that difficult world, I took deliberate steps toward my victory over cancer. The steps I will share can be used for any battle you face, not just chemo days. With that in mind, we hope the steps we took to conquer disease will help you in your healing journey.

STEP 1: PREPARE FOR MEDICATION WITH PRAYER AND MEDITATION

To counter the effects of my regular chemo infusions, I gave myself daily infusions of prayer meditations, which I called Faith Infusions for the Soul.

The psalmist said, "I will meditate on Your precepts, and contemplate Your ways" (Ps. 119:15), and that is exactly what I did. I had a list of 101 healing scriptures I spoke over myself every morning. I'd just sit there and pray and declare them. Sometimes I didn't have much energy, but I still said those scriptures out loud. On the days I had a little more energy, I declared those scriptures with a spark inside of me and did spiritual warfare.

You will find those 101 scriptures in the appendix of this book. For now, I'll share my top thirty, rock-solid favorites.

1. "Let all that I am praise the LORD; with my whole heart, I will praise his holy name. Let all that I am praise the LORD; may I never forget the good things he does for me. He forgives all my sins and heals all my diseases. He redeems me from death and crowns me with love and tender mercies. He fills my life with good things. My youth is renewed like the eagle's! The LORD gives righteousness and justice to all who are treated unfairly" (Ps. 103:1–6, NLT).

2. I declare that You are the Lord who heals me (Exod. 15:26).

3. You will remove sickness from me and give me a long, full life (Exod. 23:25–26).

4. You will protect me from *all* sickness. You will not let me suffer from the terrible diseases that people fear (Deut. 7:15).

5. You turned the intended curse into a blessing because You love me (Deut. 23:5; Neh. 13:2).

6. Christ has redeemed me from *every* curse, sickness, and plague (Gal. 3:13).

7. "As [my] days, so shall [my] strength be" (Deut. 33:25).

8. You bless me with strength and peace (Ps. 29:11).

9. You will protect me and keep me alive (Ps. 41:2).

10. You sent out Your Word and healed me, snatching me from the door of death (Ps. 107:20).

11. "I shall not die, but I shall live and declare the works of the LORD" (Ps. 118:17, MEV).

12. "The joy of the LORD is [my] strength"; "A merry heart does good like a medicine" (Neh. 8:10, MEV; Prov. 17:22, MEV).

13. "You restore my health and allow me to live!...[You are] ready to heal me!" (Isa. 38:16, 20, NLT).

14. By Your stripes I am healed (Isa. 53:5).

15. You will cause breath to enter me so I can live; You put Your Spirit in me, and I will live! (Ezek. 37:5, 14).

16. I seek You and live! (Amos 5:4, 6).

17. You are the Sun of Righteousness, and You have arisen with healing in Your wings (Mal. 4:2).

18. You took my sicknesses, and You removed my diseases (Matt. 8:17).

19. You are moved with compassion for the sick, and You heal me (Matt. 14:14).

20. You heal *every* kind of sickness and disease (Matt. 4:23).

21. *All* things are possible to me because I believe (Mark 9:23; Mark 11:23–24).

22. When hands are laid on me, *I will recover* (Mark 16:18).

23. You give me authority over all the power of the enemy, and *nothing* shall by any means hurt me (Luke 10:19).

24. If I ask anything in Your name, You will do it (John 14:14).

25. "The Spirit of God, who raised Jesus from the dead, lives in [me]. And just as God raised Christ Jesus

from the dead, he will give life to [my] mortal bodies by this same Spirit living within [me]" (Rom. 8:11, NLT).

26. I rightly discern Your body, which was broken for me, and judge myself to be saved, healed, and delivered by You; therefore, I will not be judged, I will not be weak, I will not be sickly, and I will not die prematurely (1 Cor. 11:29–31).

27. You have delivered me from death, and You will deliver me again. I place my confidence in You, and You will continue to deliver me (2 Cor. 1:10).

28. Your name is above every name, and all things are under Your feet, including sickness. I am seated with You in heavenly places, and *all things* are under my feet (Phil. 2:8–11; Eph. 1:21–22; 2:6).

29. Your Word says that by Your stripes (wounds) I was healed; *therefore, I am healed* (1 Pet. 2:24).

30. Your "divine power has given to [me] *all things* that pertain to life and godliness through the knowledge of [You] who has called [me] by [Your] own glory and excellence" (2 Pet. 1:3, MEV).

STEP 2: PRAISE, WORSHIP, AND SING VICTORY SONGS

The hours before chemo and even on the drive to the chemo infusion center, I filled the atmosphere with worship. My smartphone was always playing worship songs like "How Great Thou Art," "Raise a Hallelujah," and "Surrounded (Fight My Battles)." There were other songs too.

Psalm 149:6 says, "Let the high praises of God be in their mouth, and a two-edged sword in their hand." I made a point of singing only happy, joyful praise songs that would perk me up, and I avoided sad songs, sad movies, and sad stories. I disciplined myself to stay in a positive state of mind. Sometimes I sang with boldness and put my foot down in dominion over disease and sickness. Other times I sang slowly and deliberately, dwelling on God's goodness and power. Still other times I would literally pause and "be still, and *know* that [He is] God" (Ps. 46:10, emphasis added).

STEP 3: KNOW THAT YOUR SMILE BECOMES YOU

Sometimes we smile because we're happy. Sometimes we're happy because we smile. I've said and taught this for nearly half a century. It was my choice on chemo day to smile—to try to be a blessing and a light. Scripture tells us the Lord Himself is our light and the help of our countenance.

> The LORD lift up His countenance upon you, and give you peace.
> —NUMBERS 6:26

> LORD, lift up the light of Your countenance upon us.
> —PSALM 4:6

When I say, "Your smile becomes you," I mean that in a quite literal way. A smile lights up our face and can light up a room, someone else's life, or even the world.

I'd deliberately walk into my appointments with my head high, keeping in mind the psalmist's words: "But You, O LORD, are a shield for me, my glory and the One who lifts up my head" (Ps. 3:3).

Remember, your smile becomes you. As we choose to put on joy and a smile by faith, it becomes real and genuine. The joy of the Lord is our strength—literally!

STEP 4: RISE UP ABOVE YOUR CIRCUMSTANCES—"I AM NOT A VICTIM"

In sports you may hear a coach say, "Time to get our game face on!" I've had to do that, and I even have a slogan I use to encourage myself. It's not "Fake it till you make it" but "*Faith* it till you make it!"

Pressing into a realm of faith is not only about spiritual warfare. Our spirit and our emotions are tightly wound together. God created us in His image; we are made up of spirit, mind, and body. I made it my goal to get all three of these components together before my next chemo infusion.

My daughters Katie and/or Anna took me to all my infusion appointments, stayed with me, and drove me home afterward. All the way there, we played our favorite worship songs, sang, and declared God's promises.

Before we left the house, I would dress in a cute, comfortable outfit; running shoes; and cheery inspirational butterfly jewelry. I'd draw on eyebrows (since mine fell out) and eyeliner (since my eyelashes fell out too) and put on suntan-color foundation, bronzer, and blush to brighten up my pale facial skin. Then I'd apply under-eye concealer to cover the dark, heavy circles under my eyes. A bright lipstick color helped my smile, but I didn't have any hair to style, so I'd cover my bald head with a sassy ball cap and pack up my supplies—my Bible and headphones. Last, I'd put on my big faith smile. Now I could look in the mirror and see my familiar, healthy self!

Katie, Larry, Anna, and I would meet in the kitchen and take smiling victory pictures. We'd have our prayer of faith together, and Larry would cover me in God's promises of divine health and protection. Then he'd give me a big hug and kiss and walk Katie and me to the car.

I'd tell him, "Bye-bye! We are off to another day at the spa!"

Why did I go to all this trouble just to get a chemo infusion? I did anything and everything I could not to see myself as a victim of cancer. The face I saw first thing each morning was not a pretty sight. If I looked exhausted and sick, it made me feel worse. I always feel better when I fix myself up. It picks up my spirit and brings out the best in me.

"As [a man] thinks in his heart, so is he" (Prov. 23:7, MEV). It is critical and essential to do all we can to envision ourselves whole and healed as an act of faith. I didn't allow myself to get stuck in the muck. I made the choice to rejoice. I was not trying to convince anyone but myself that I was not going to become a victim of cancer or of circumstances.

STEP 5: GUARD YOUR HEART

I once read a quote that said, "All the water in the oceans cannot sink a ship unless it gets inside."[1]

In human terms, all the oceans of trauma cannot sink your ship unless they get inside you. Don't let yourself go there. Stay on the sunny side of life.

Do not google every new treatment someone tells you about. Let God lead your research. Pay attention to what voices you allow to speak into your life.

Saturate your soul with what God says about you and your circumstances, not what the world predicts. When going through a serious trial, you must be careful what you hear and who you have around you. Even well-meaning and caring people can sometimes express their compassion in a way that leaves a person feeling down. Of course, we don't want to be rude or insensitive, but it's important to be firm in creating emotional boundaries and shielding ourselves from negativity.

During this battle, there were times when we were emotionally drained and struggling to keep our heads above water. We had to apologize for not ministering at our usual capacity and explained why we had to isolate at times. Boundaries are necessary as you "faith it till you make it." It may seem extreme, but for me it was a matter of life and death.

STEP 6: AVOID NEGATIVE TALK AND CONVERSATIONS

Give yourself permission to be selective in your social life. Give yourself permission to take care of and focus on yourself for a period of time. When people hear about your struggle, they all want to tell you their stories and experiences. Sorry, but we can only afford to hear the victories, miracles, and success stories. There is power in the words you allow into your conversation and thought life. Put your guard up!

It may seem impossible to stay positive in conversation when you are dealing with a health issue that must be monitored each month. Blood work, tumor markers, physical progress, emotional stability, and worsening symptoms all were assessed on a regular basis.

There are ways to deal with life's genuine realities without diving into negativity. Early in our marriage, Larry and I developed a pattern for discussing real-life issues that came up while keeping faith-filled attitudes. You can state the reality of the negative report and follow it up by saying, "Let's pray about that right now." Or you may decide to search the Scriptures together for a promise to declare that pertains to that bad report.

Faith and common sense do not cancel each other out. In fact, they can and should work together to bring great success and breakthroughs. As our family processed and walked through the reports, stats, and treatments, we assessed it all, chose options, and then covered everything in prayer and wrapped it in God's promises. Again, let me emphasize that we were not denying the reality of our pain or negative circumstances, but we were denying their right to rule and reign in our future!

STEP 7: DON'T RUN FROM THE TEARS

It's OK to allow yourself to have a good cry. At times I would let it all out and then rein in that sad feeling and rise up, knowing that one day I would reap in joy, as the Scriptures say.

Those who sow in tears shall reap in joy.

—Psalm 126:5

You number my wanderings; put my tears into Your bottle; are they not in Your book?

—Psalm 56:8

Remember, the same hands that hold the universe in place hold our lives in place too. Joy will come in the morning.

Those few days before infusion day, my emotions would try to go to the dark side and into the deep waters. I had to stay afloat. I had to be strong for my family and our congregation, and they had to be strong for me. No sad songs, no sad movies, no sad stories, no sad memories, no sad conversations. We put ourselves on a strict diet of positive, happy, victorious, faith-infused influences.

That being said, there is also something amazingly powerful and healing about crying. Numerous medical studies have concluded that emotional tears (as opposed to tears from cutting onions, allergies, or the wind) contain feel-good chemicals such as oxytocin and endogenous opioids (endorphins) that help relieve both physical and emotional pain. Emotional tears also flush out stress hormones and other toxins that accumulate in our bodies.[2]

I once read a quote attributed to Karl Menninger that said, "Weeping is perhaps the most human and universal of all relief measures."[3] It amazes me that God Himself created this incredible function in our human bodies. Weeping is much more than a random reaction to emotional and physical pain. It is part of God's way of bringing relief and healing to our heart, soul, and body.

My motto and advice is this: Have a good old cry and let it all out—either alone with God or on someone's shoulder. Then dry your tears and get on with life!

STEP 8: LAUGH

You've probably heard statistics that laughter releases the same endorphins released when the body is healing itself. It's true.[4] Sorrows run deep at times, but so do joy and laughter. Sometimes laughing turns into crying, and sometimes crying turns into laughter.

The Bible encourages us to be joyful.

> But let all those rejoice who put their trust in You; let them ever shout for joy, because You defend them; let those also who love Your name be joyful in You.
>
> —PSALM 5:11

> Make me hear joy and gladness.
>
> —PSALM 51:8

It is healing to hear laughter and the joyful sounds of loved ones. So many times in our family, when painful emotions are ready to burst, one of us will deliberately say something funny, causing us all to belly laugh rather than sob. Our deep human emotions seem to come from the same place and manifest in tears or laughter. Being able to find humor and laughter during deeply stressful times is truly a gift that bonds, heals, and creates memories for a lifetime.

MAKING PEACE WITH THE PROCESS

As I've said before, my family and I sure would have loved it if God had just done one giant miracle to remove cancer from me and leukemia from Lion as soon as we were diagnosed. Instead, He saw us through by providing big and small miracles by the moment that added up to our giant miracles of victory. Glory to God!

The world we live in is one of immediate gratification and quick resolutions, which lead to short attention spans and a lack of endurance. Jam-packed schedules are daily realities for most of us, including me. Getting my head around the procedures and commitments that accompanied a cancer diagnosis was an entire issue in and of itself. Coming to terms with these protracted disruptions to my life, health, schedule, and foreseeable future created stress, frustration, and irritation. In some ways this became even more challenging over time. In the beginning I mustered up everything within me to rise to the challenges, but as time went on I grew weary and frustrated. I just wanted my life to be normal again. I had to dig deep and come to terms with what I call "the long run."

At a chemo appointment I saw a brochure titled "Making Peace With Cancer." My gut reaction was anger; I didn't ever want to make peace with cancer or stop warring against it. But in time I realized this brochure was not referring to making peace with cancer itself but with everything that came along with it. It was encouraging me to find peace in the midst of it all.

In 2 Corinthians 12, the apostle Paul tells of struggling with a tormenting thorn in his flesh. Scripture does not reveal what the thorn was, but Paul pleaded with God three times to take it away. The Lord did not remove it, but He said, "My grace is sufficient for you, for My strength is made perfect in weakness" (v. 9, MEV). I have taught often on this scripture and how the Lord has met me at various points of my needs through the years.

The Lord's response to Paul's prayer has many layers of interpretation and application. I've heard it taught that God's unwillingness to remove the thorn was a rebuke, implying that Paul was asking for too much and needed to just "deal with it and get over it." But I don't believe God was telling Paul that he was asking too *much* from Him. Rather, I believe God was telling him that His grace was already *more* than enough to enable Paul to rise above, overcome, and conquer the tormenting challenge he faced. Paul just needed to recognize this and tap into it.

GOD'S GRACE IS MORE THAN ENOUGH

I've always believed that no matter what we are facing, God's grace, equipping, and empowering are more than enough to see us through. Sometimes the Lord delivered His people *out* of darkness and trouble. Sometimes He led them *through* the darkness and trouble. Think about Moses leading the Israelites through the desert away from the violent armies pursuing them. When they came to the Red Sea, they faced an insurmountable problem. The Lord could have saved them in innumerable, miraculous ways, including by drying up or removing the life-threatening sea. Instead of *removing* the sea, the Lord parted the waters and led them *through* the sea. Like Paul, each one of us needs to learn how to tap into the reality of God's never-ending, all-sufficient help.

I adopted the habit of continually giving my impatience, frustrations, weariness, and anxieties to the Lord. I found myself asking Him daily for an extra-large dose of grace to help me *through* the long run.

I did not and will not make peace with the cancer. But I did make peace with the process it took to get through it—and I made it my habit to embrace the grace!

I'M NOT WORRYING, BUT I AM WARRING

In the days that followed the ovarian cancer diagnosis, hundreds of worrisome thoughts rushed through my mind. Of course, I had to process many details of what was ahead of me. Faith doesn't mean we ignore the doctor's instructions or bury our heads in the sand. There were real issues to deal with. As I figured out many details, I made sure to view them through the lens of God's promises.

A thought came to my mind that became one of my mottos: *I'm not worrying, but I am warring!*

At all times, no matter what phase of life we are in or what we are going through, we need to practice having faith and being positive. I do this by reminding myself of the following:

I will:

- saturate my mind, soul, and heart with God's promises;

- settle in my mind that I can trust Him and His promises;

- reframe my mindset from negative to positive;

- give myself an attitude adjustment;

- give myself a checkup from the neck up;

- realize that my own self-talk is the most important conversation of the day;

- reframe my challenges through the Word of God;

- refocus my future through the lens of God's promises;

- face my day "in-couraged";

- not face my day "dis-couraged"—the absence of courage;

- arrest and block the negative, downward spiral of doubt and fear;

- release a positive, faith-fueled spiral of hope and courage;

- remember I am more than a conqueror through Him who loves me (Rom. 8:37);

- remind myself that I am not worrying, but I am warring; and

- choose to believe that despite all these things, overwhelming victory is mine through Christ, who loves me (Rom. 8:37–39).

WHEN KATIE AND I SMILED

As I mentioned, my daughters Katie and/or Anna always went with me to the infusions. One day when Katie was going to go with me, some of my numbers were not as good as the previous month, which raised some concern. We covered it in prayer and headed to the cancer center.

The infusion treatment center was very crowded. We found an open chair, and the nurse hooked me up to the IV for infusion. As you can imagine, there are a lot of stressed faces in an infusion center, and it's a pretty somber, quiet atmosphere. We always made a point to focus our attention not on those around us but on each other and keep our emotions and hopes high. We began calling these medical infusions my "faith infusions" because we used that time to build our faith, even sharing praise reports of people in our congregation. Sometimes we listened to new worship songs or faith-filled messages.

I felt nauseated that day and a bit shaken from the blood test results. I was battling a heavy heart, and although she didn't say so, I knew Katie was too.

As we settled in, Katie told me about several people in our church who were getting blessed or healed or having other good things happen to them. As we talked, we got excited—not loud, but happy.

After about a half hour, a woman got up from across the room and headed right to us. I thought maybe she was going to tell us to quiet down so we wouldn't disturb other patients. Instead, she gave us a big smile, leaned down, and asked us, "What's the story on you two? I'm here with my sister, who's getting her infusion, and we've been watching you both. Your joy and spirit are lighting up the room! At first we thought the sun was shining in from the window and lighting up your faces. Then we realized you are not in the sun. You're in the shadows. The light is not shining on you. It's shining out from within you! What is your story?"

Katie and I told her we were believers and talked with her about our faith and our God.

She said, "Well, whatever you've got, we need some of it too!"

We were able to tell her about the Lord and pray with her and her sister for God's touch and miraculous intervention.

MAGNIFY THE LORD, NOT CIRCUMSTANCES

Psalm 34:3 says, "Oh, magnify the LORD with me." Magnification doesn't change what we are looking at; it just enlarges it. It focuses on and accentuates it. When we look at God and magnify Him, we are focusing on and enlarging His attributes.

Psalm 34:3 also says, "Let us exalt His name." His name is Healer, and His power is larger than the events going on in the world or the circumstances in our lives. To exalt means to glorify, praise, and lift up above everything else. Let's choose to elevate God and His promises above any challenges we're facing. Instead of magnifying the problems in the world, magnify the promises in His Word.

I'm telling you the story about the chemo day because it made such an impact on Katie and me. We were weary and a bit shaken up, but we chose to rise above it in faith and tap into God's strength. We "put on" faith and joy and deliberately magnified the Lord rather than the negative reports and down feelings. We weren't particularly aware of having an extra touch from the Holy Spirit, but I do remember our hearts being lifted as we talked about the goodness of God.

This is another example of God's miracles by the moment. As Katie and I faced the distressing reports, we made the choice to rejoice once again. The Spirit of God filled us, equipped us, and brought healing to our hearts, minds, and bodies. By the way, it took another month to confirm, but the next time my blood work was checked, those numbers that troubled us were back to normal *and improving.* It was another miracle by the moment!

When the woman told us how we appeared to her, Katie and I

realized how in-the-moment our God is. He met us at the point of our need, and He can do the same for you too.

MY ATTITUDE FORMULA

This story of what happened when Katie and I chose to smile exemplifies the entirety of our journey. Let me put my daily formula into an easy to-do list:

1. Rise up thanking God for waking me and giving me life, health, strength, equipping, direction, wisdom, peace, love, and joy.

2. Breathe in His breath of life and let it fill my being.

3. Smile at the Lord. Love on Him. Sense His smile and love right back at me. Feel His presence and reality.

4. Focus on my God, His love, and His greatness before I focus on my to-do list and challenges.

5. Cover and fill my mind, heart, soul, and body with His Holy Spirit, promises, blessings, and miracles.

6. Determine that no matter what the day brings, the Lord already has it all covered and taken care of. He's got this, so I've got this!

7. Put on happy clothes, happy makeup, a happy attitude, happy thoughts, and a happy smile. Carry myself like I'm already healed, whole, and victorious.

8. Remember that my smile becomes me. Sometimes we smile because we're happy; sometimes we're happy because we smile.

9. Ask God to not only bless me and my family but to use me to be a blessing to others. We are blessed to be a blessing!

10. Make the choice to rejoice—then repeat, repeat, repeat. The joy of the Lord is my strength!

11. Rise above negative circumstances with positive thoughts, words, and actions. Take the high road.

12. Be the light! Be the blessing! Be the bringer of joy! Giving has a boomerang effect. What we cause to happen for others, God will cause to happen for us.

13. Joy + Faith = Miracles by the Moment.

14. If I mess up, fall short, or completely blow it, I shout, "Grace!" I immediately ask forgiveness from the Lord and the person I hurt, if applicable, then I get up, get over it, and get on with it.

15. Repeat this formula and smile!

CHAPTER 7

MIRACLE MOMENTS ADD UP TO ONE GIANT MIRACLE

TIZ HUCH

I LOVE IT WHEN someone gets their miracle right away or receives prayer one night and wakes up healed the next morning. I praise God for that! Sometimes breakthrough comes in the form of one giant miracle. Most of the time, many smaller miracles add up to the giant miracle.

I want to share several miracle moments that led up to my final healing. Then I want to share the miracle of Lion's healing.

OPERATION EAGLE'S WINGS

Larry and I were supposed to be in Israel on July 17, 2019, to celebrate Operation Eagle's Wings—the name Israel gave to helping Ethiopian Jews make their *aliyah* to Israel. The word *aliyah* means the return or immigration of Jews to Israel. Oftentimes Jewish people make their aliyah to escape antisemitism or persecution. We've helped save thousands of lives by supporting aliyah efforts.

On July 17, 2019, two giant planeloads of Jewish Ethiopians that our ministry helped sponsor were on their way to Israel, and we were so excited! Prime Minister Benjamin Netanyahu and his wife, Sara, along with other members of the Israeli government were to meet at the airport to greet and welcome the Ethiopian Jews upon their arrival. Larry was to be the keynote speaker, and we were thrilled to be taking part in such a huge, life-changing event.

One week before our trip to Israel, we were on the way to church, and Larry said, "Tiz, why don't you receive the offering this morning?"

I said, "Great! I woke up with Psalm 103 on my heart."

That morning I taught our congregation about praise, thanksgiving and expectation of God's blessings and benefits as I quoted Psalm 103:2–5:

> Bless the LORD, O my soul, and forget not all His benefits: who forgives all your iniquities, who heals all your diseases, who redeems your life from destruction, who crowns you with lovingkindness and tender mercies, who satisfies your mouth with good things, so that your youth is renewed like the eagle's.

While speaking, it occurred to me that, as we were about to go to Israel to celebrate Operation Eagle's Wings, I was quoting Scripture about our youth being renewed like the eagle's. I felt an extra unction as I made this connection, and our people felt it too. I had no idea, however, that this scripture that the Lord impressed on my heart was for me and would be my own promise to myself in the upcoming events.

Bless the Lord and remember all His benefits! Forgiveness, healing, delivers from destruction, lovingkindness and mercies, satisfies my mouth with good things, renews my youth (health) like the eagles—those were all some benefits that I was about to have need of!

One week later, which could only be by God's orchestration, my operation was scheduled for July 17—the very same day Israel's Operation Eagle's Wings brought home two planeloads of Ethiopian Jews. We all felt encouraged that God's hand was on both operations. Although I had to miss out on Operation Eagle's Wings' meeting the planes in Israel, I had my very own

Operation Eagle's Wings in the oncology surgical ward—meeting with the Lord!

MY JOURNEY TO THE ONCOLOGIST

The previous month, Larry and I led a tour group of one hundred people in Israel. During that trip, in early June, I began to feel something wasn't quite right in my abdomen area. When we got home, I made an appointment to see a doctor who specializes in digestive disorders, and the appointment just happened to be the day after that amazing church service.

I explained my symptoms, and the doctor sent me to have a CT scan the following day. It normally takes two to three days to get the results of those scans, but the doctor called me two hours after I'd had the scan done and had me get an ultrasound. A day after the ultrasound, the doctor called and said, "I'm sending you to a gynecologist for an ultrasound and then to a gynecological oncologist. I see things that are suspicious, and it's out of my league. I already called and made the way."

I had never met this doctor before, but he got me through to the top oncologist in our area in just a few days. Larry, Anna, and Katie went with me, but I wasn't even really worried about it.

The oncologist said, "I don't need a biopsy. I saw the CT scan and the ultrasound. I know what it is. It's ovarian cancer and very advanced. This is extremely serious and urgent. I've cleared my schedule to do surgery on you in three days."

We didn't know this oncologist, but we knew people often waited months to see a specialist like this. Yet he cleared his schedule and was able to do surgery in three days. *Three days.*

Right away I protested. We were to be in Israel again in three days for Operation Eagle's Wings. We were scheduled to meet several planeloads of Jewish people from Ethiopia whom we had sponsored to immigrate to Israel. We would finally get to meet and hug the people we were helping to escape persecution. My first reaction was to say this event was too important to miss and the surgery could wait until we got back.

But the oncologist said, "Mrs. Huch, the most important thing on your agenda is this surgery. I'm sure everyone in the room feels this way right now."

"Absolutely," Larry agreed. "I'll call them right now and cancel our trip."

And he did.

Larry and I canceled our trip to Israel, and I had surgery instead. We sensed that God's hand was on both *operations*. I felt God's Spirit surrounding me, and I knew in my heart that the Lord's hand was on my surgeon, just as His hand was on Operation Eagle's Wings. Looking back, Larry and I know the timing was no coincidence. On the very same day God was saving the lives of two planeloads of persecuted Ethiopian Jews by bringing them to their homeland through Operation Eagle's Wings, He was using the skill of the surgeon to save my life.

The oncologist operated on me for eight hours and took out seven organs. He said the cancer was like grains of sand throughout my body, and he got every single piece he could. He said the cancer probably had been in there for only one or two months—just about as long as I'd had the unusual pains in my abdomen. I oftentimes put medical things off, and part of my miracle is that even with the Israel trip coming up, I didn't put off my appointment. My oncologist said I may have lived only two or three months had I not seen a doctor when I did. The cancer had spread quickly in just a month or two.

Part of this miracle was how quickly the doctors got me in and scheduled the surgery. I later learned that my oncologist is one of the most sought after in the Dallas metroplex. He has surgeries scheduled months out, yet he operated on me within three days of my appointment with him. Honestly, before I even knew I needed a miracle, God already set me on the journey to healing.

Because of his extreme rush to operate, the oncologist said he really wouldn't know the full extent of the cancer until he had me in surgery and could see everything. We prayed with him for God to bless and equip him with godly wisdom, guidance, strength, peace, and expertise—not only for my surgery but for all the surgeries he performs.

MAJOR SURGERY, MAJOR MIRACLES

Before surgery, the cancer number in my body was nearly four hundred. Immediately after surgery it was down to thirty. Anything thirty and below is considered normal. I was cancer-free. My cancer numbers went from extremely high to normal after an eight-hour surgery. That is astounding!

My oncologist was amazed and overwhelmingly pleased with the results. He told us this outcome was not typical. In most cases, even after extensive surgery, there is still measurable cancer in the body because surgeons cannot get to all of it to remove it. In my case, the doctor was worried that the cancer had spread so extensively through my organs and tissues that it would not be operable or containable. He gratefully acknowledged that our prayers had helped him in my operation. He also said the Lord played a huge role in the outcome. While the surgeon was operating on me in the natural realm, God was operating on me in the supernatural realm! He verified orally and on paper proven results that I was cancer-free! Glory to God!

PHASE 2

The thing about cancer is that if even a tiny molecule of it is left in any part of your body, it will race back in an even greater way than in the beginning. That meant I had to go through six months of chemotherapy to ensure every trace of the cancer was eradicated.

After the surgery I had no detectable cancer in my body, but medically they won't declare you cancer-free until you've gone through a full chemo process and been tested again afterward. Considering that, the results of the surgery were huge.

TIZ'S GENE MIRACLE

Every single month after July 2019, I had a follow-up oncology appointment. Whether I was receiving chemo or in other phases of treatment, I had blood work and tests done to measure my progress and healing. At these monthly checkups, the cancer numbers in my body have never gone above thirty-three, and the cancer hasn't grown or spread in three years. Those were more miracles by the moment. My monthly checkups, blood work, and CT scans confirmed undeniably what we already knew—I was healed.

However, my testing was not over. Within a few months the oncologist sent me for tests to determine whether I had the BRCA gene mutation. With any type of female cancer, they do genetic testing to document your genetic history and find out who had cancer in your family. There were many women and men in my family who'd had cancer, so from my oncologist's point of view, it was a no-brainer that I had the dreaded BRCA gene mutation. This mutation puts you at greater risk of developing breast or ovarian cancer.

The more I learned about it, the more likely it seemed that I had the BRCA gene mutation. This is the frightening way I saw it: If you have the BRCA gene mutation, then you are swimming upstream, trying to outswim cancer for the rest of your life. It increases the likelihood of the cancer returning, and worse, you have a one-in-two chance of passing the gene on to your children.[1]

The oncologist was certain I had the BRCA gene mutation. The worst thing I faced throughout my journey was waiting those three weeks for the test results. I gave them a long list of relatives who either had cancer or died from cancer. To think I could pass this horrible disease on to my daughters, son, and grandchildren was more devastating to me than having cancer.

I thought, "Was it my BRCA gene that caused Lion to have this cancer?" It was the worst feeling. What do you do? We went to war.

No way was the BRCA gene mutation going to manifest in my family. This took our warfare to an even higher level. Beyond fighting for my own life, now I was fighting for the lives of my daughters, son, and grandkids. A righteous indignation rose inside of me, and I said, "No way!"

MY GREATEST BREAKTHROUGH

As a family, we went to war. We broke generational curses.

The oncologist called me in after two weeks and said, "I know you have BRCA gene mutation, but your results say you don't. So I'm having everything retested. I'm sending biopsies of organs we took out and retesting."

This was important because the treatment would be different depending on the test results. If I had the BRCA gene mutation, then all my kids, grandkids, and siblings would have to be tested too and consider preventive treatments or therapies.

I couldn't believe I had to wait another three weeks for the test results. The weight of it was so heavy.

My girls said, "Mom, even if the test is positive, God's going to break that generational spirit."

Three weeks later the oncologist said, "I'm baffled, but you don't have the BRCA gene mutation. Honestly, I'm at a loss as to what to do with you. I want to treat you in a preventive way, but medically if I don't have proof you have the BRCA gene mutation, I can't treat you that way."

What he was saying was that he wanted to get to the root and source of this thing. Yet all of that double testing still proved conclusively that I did not have the BRCA gene mutation.

As we walked out of his office that day, the specialist who conducted all my DNA testing pulled me into her office. She pointed to a plaque on her wall that said, "With God, Nothing Is Impossible." She whispered, "This could only, *only* be God." She knew what my doctor knew. With my family history and symptoms, the intense testing should have revealed the dreaded BRCA gene mutation, but it did not!

Without a doubt, I'm convinced God broke that generational curse of cancer. God eliminated the BRCA gene mutation that had stolen the lives of my relatives. That BRCA gene mutation would not steal my life, nor would it threaten the lives of my family's future generations. What a *huge* miracle—and it's documented medically, proof that our God performs miracles!

RING THE BELL!

After six months of chemo, the oncologist put me on an immunotherapy treatment. I still had appointments every month for two years until January 2022. Each month, I had full blood work done, and I had CT scans every three months. July 2022 marked three years since my diagnosis, and the cancer is still completely gone and my health is fantastic!

Each month of testing confirmed what we already knew by faith—God completely healed me. I am right at three years since the initial surgery, and I am cancer-free! Glory to God!

We did absolutely everything we could in the natural and medical realms. But, as I said, these victory reports are not the norm. Our God is a miracle-working God!

When a cancer patient finishes chemo, they ring the bell. When the day came that I got to ring the bell, Anna and Katie were with me. I didn't ring it once; I rang it nonstop for over a minute. Everyone was laughing—nurses, everyone. It was crazy! I was celebrating and declaring a huge marker in my healing miracle journey! Now, as I tell my story to you, I am ringing the bell for the world to hear that what the Lord has done for Lion and me He can do for you too! I don't tell this story to draw attention to myself but to my God! Nothing is too hard for Him!

LION'S JOURNEY

We are a close family. All our kids work with us in the ministry, and we live within a few minutes of each other. Lion's diagnosis was not only emotionally devastating for us but so out of order for our faith. There was no way this was supposed to happen.

I explained earlier how the hospital moved Lion, with Jen and Luke, to the oncology floor and started chemo on him that very day. He had blood work daily, and the chemo was as intense as an infant could tolerate. The medical team searched worldwide for outside medical records and reports that could give them insight into such a rare form of leukemia. They told us it was extremely rare for a child of seven months to have that type of leukemia. Worse, there was not one record of an infant who had survived that type of leukemia.

We were told there was a particular gene that seemed to make a difference in survival rates. Lion's oncologist told Luke, Jen, and the rest of us, "The medical world doesn't know much about this form of leukemia in an infant because it is so rare. We'll run another series of tests that will help us determine his outcome. If he has this certain negative gene, it will decrease his chances of survival significantly."

We all waited anxiously, praying for those test results. When they finally came back, the oncologists said they needed to do further testing. So we waited and prayed for weeks for news about whether or not Lion had this negative gene.

LION'S GENE MIRACLE

After such intense waiting, the doctor came with a report. He said, "Listen, I don't understand this. We ran these tests numerous times to be sure we were seeing this accurately. Lion does not have the negative gene. That's great news! What's more, he has a positive gene that is present in children only when they enter their teenage years." At seven months old, Lion had a positive gene in his body that shifted his chance of survival from very low to very high!

Glory to God! There is no record anywhere in the world of a child under the age of puberty-onset having this positive gene. This gene helps the body fight off infection and blood disease. Having this positive gene at such an early age was an absolute game changer for our grandson.

The chemo treatments continued, and over time the spinal taps, blood work, and tests all showed that the leukemia was decreasing even as his health and numbers "trended upward." That is the medical term for getting better. This term became a daily statement of our faith and prayer declarations. In addition to God's steady flow of huge miracles, we asked for and saw His supernatural help, healing, and hope continually "trend upward." Miracles by the moment!

It was a giant miracle that Lion had that positive gene, as the medical community had no record of an infant ever having that gene in the entire world.

The oncologists and nurses overseeing Lion's treatment were all astounded and agreed that only God could have done this. There was no explanation, precedent, or case in the world where this had taken place. There was no way, in the natural or medical field, this could take place. This truly had to be a miracle from God!

GOD IS IN CHARGE OF MIRACLES

With Lion, God miraculously put in a helpful gene. With me, He miraculously took out a harmful gene. God is in charge of His miracles, and He is in charge of their timing too.

This put a new meaning and relevance to the scripture "The LORD gave, and the LORD has taken away" (Job 1:21)! We do our best, and God does the rest. We do all we can in the natural realm, but then God adds His super to our natural!

The leukemia decreased in Lion's blood, and within two years he was completely fine, finished with chemo, and totally cancer-free and healthy!

As a family we shared in the great miracle of peace in the storm, joy in the journey, closeness as a family, and closeness to the Lord. Our faith increased as we magnified God above all during a time when we could have gotten discouraged. Instead, we kept our eyes on the Lord, and our faith grew.

The verse I clung to throughout this three-year journey is

Deuteronomy 33:25—"as your days, so shall your strength be." I used this verse over and over again to take the next step and then the next.

If you or a loved one has cancer, then you know people don't get cancer. Families get cancer. It was extremely hard for me to see my kids and grandkids go through this. But I can testify that God helped my children and grandchildren, and as a mother that's important to me.

Larry and I have lived by Romans 8:28 for nearly fifty years. We know that all things work together for good, and if something didn't work out quite right, it didn't matter what came our way because we knew God was bigger. He would work out everything for His good and ours too.

For every mountain, there's a miracle.

For every problem, there's a promise.

Even when we don't see Him or feel Him, He is working on our behalf to turn our darkness into light and our aches into beauty.

God has already worked out the details for our good. Glory to God!

CHAPTER 8

YOU ARE NOT ALONE
TIZ HUCH

HAVE YOU EVER felt all alone in a crowded room? I have. I'm writing this chapter to assure you that you are not alone. *You are on God's mind and heart right now.*

Psalm 115:12–13 says, "The LORD hath been mindful of us: he will bless us...both small and great" (KJV). That's incredible, isn't it? You are on His mind right now! Realizing that you are not alone is actually the first step to entering into God's unlimited promises and miracles.

King David writes in Psalm 139 that God's thoughts about us outnumber the grains of sand on the seashore. Wow! Look at this:

> How precious also are Your thoughts to me, O God! How great is the sum of them! If I should count them, they would be more in number than the sand; when I awake, I am still with You.
>
> —PSALM 139:17–18

Have you ever had someone reach out to you and tell you they had been thinking about you or praying for you? This is what God Himself is saying to you right here. He has you on His mind right now! He is thinking about you when you lie down, and He is thinking about you when you wake up.

Without question, the Lord desires to have an intimate,

ongoing relationship with each of us. His desire is to bless us in every way and in every area of our lives.

REALLY—GOD IS THINKING ABOUT YOU

Jeremiah 29:11 says, "For I know the thoughts that I think toward you...thoughts of peace, and not of evil, to give you an expected end" (KJV). Think about that. God Himself has made plans for you—good plans, not evil plans. Knowing this is a game changer in how we view ourselves, our lives, and our futures.

The circumstances of life can sometimes make it seem as if the walls are closing in around us. We can feel overwhelmed by responsibilities, financial pressures, and negative health reports. Tumultuous events going on in the world or even within our own families can send us spinning into a whirlwind of emotions and fears. At times we feel like we're carrying the weight of the world on our shoulders all by ourselves, with no one to help us. If we give our attention and faith to those reports and events, they can take us into a downward spiral of hopelessness.

I want to tell you again right now that you are not alone. No matter where you are in life, no matter how enormous your challenges are, no matter how many times you think you've messed up or failed, and no matter how dire the medical reports and statistics are, God is at this very moment thinking about you. He cares for you, and He is mapping out a fabulous, amazing future for you.

You're not the only one who wants your life and circumstances to change for the better. Your God wants them to change for the better too. Even better news—He has mapped out specific, daily ways for you to accomplish this and step into your victories. Before you even knew you had a challenge, God had already worked out His answers.

PANDEMIC SHUTDOWNS AND CHALLENGES

From 2020 until 2022, nearly every person on earth was affected to one degree or another by the deadly virus COVID-19. Statistics tell us that millions of people worldwide have died from contracting COVID-19. Talk about feeling alone! This disease threw our world into a panic, and we've all suffered from lockdowns, social isolation, stress, grief, and uncertainty. Many have had to maneuver job loss, school closings, grocery shortages, decisions about whether to wear a mask, financial instability, and, worse, the loss of a friend or loved one. If you watch the news, the heaviness of the COVID pandemic tends to flow into the room. Fears, depression, and isolation try to settle on our emotions like a thick layer of fog, increasing mental health issues among our human family.

The constant barrage of bad news, financial fears, misinformation, and outright lies leaves us longing for honest answers. But we constantly hear, "This is our new normal." We long for and hope that life will return to the *old* normal.

Although I've talked about feeling all alone in a crowded room, most of us haven't been in too many crowded rooms these past few years at all. Quarantines, isolation, and shutdowns have left us hungry and longing for social interaction. Much of our time has been spent not in crowded rooms but all alone in our living rooms!

I don't want to cast doom and gloom or focus on bad news. I'm just creating the backdrop for us to look at God's hope, promises, and *good* news.

Even in the best of times, life can be full of uncertainties. Faith, prayer, and trust in God are not just for people in tough times; they are for all people, at all times!

BE A BLESSING

Even when the world seems to be in perfect order, we can experience feelings of loneliness with no one to lean on. However, it's an even greater blessing to *be* that support person in another person's life. No matter how divided, computerized, or separated our world becomes, people need people.

I always tell people, "If you need a friend, *be* a friend." Proverbs 18:24 says, "A man who has friends must himself be friendly." Let me tell you a quick-tip fix to loneliness. Don't fall into the trap of self-pity or feeling alone. If we wait around for people to reach out to us, we may wait a long, lonely time. How about rising up and becoming the person who reaches out and becomes a friend and encourager to others? During our tough times in the hospitals and cancer centers, it was easy to feel sad, alone, and sorry for ourselves. To counter this, we chose to be the light bringers to others by smiling, caring, and speaking hope into their lives.

When we cheer up others, we ultimately cheer up ourselves. Love and kindness are like boomerangs that always return back to us. Sometimes the most spiritual thing we can do is be a friend to someone.

We need to be loved, and we need to *give* love. In those relationships we find wholeness and purpose for our own lives. We are blessed to *be* a blessing! Yet the Bible tells us in 1 John 4:19, "We love Him because He first loved us."

The beginning of all love is God. Always remember God loves you, and He is longing to spend time with you today and even more time with you tomorrow. He longs to talk to you and listen to you and be your best friend.

GOD WANTS TO BE WITH YOU

Recently I received a text from a business associate I hadn't seen or heard from in months. After our short conversation about a business matter, I asked how she and her family were doing. She texted that they had gone through a rough time for the past few months with COVID-19 running through their family of seven people. She said it was very scary and had compounded their financial problems because they couldn't work their jobs. She said they were still getting back on their feet. I told her that Larry and I would pray for them for God's healing, financial recovery, and blessings.

She responded, "Thank you so much. I'm so thankful we all made it through. But I feel like the Lord has His hands full with much more important problems going on all over the world right now. We are probably the least of His concerns. But thank you for your kind words and prayers."

This is indicative of how most people really feel about God and His feelings toward them.

At one time or another, most of us have experienced feeling unaccepted or unloved. And if we're truthful, sometimes we aren't exactly lovable, are we? If our friends and family members occasionally don't even want to be with us, why would God Almighty want to hang out with us?

Do you find it difficult to fathom that God takes pleasure in spending time with you? Why would He want to commune with us flawed and fallen human beings? Think about the Garden of Eden and the very first people. In short, from the very beginning God has always wanted a family. He loved coming to the Garden of Eden and talking to Adam and Eve in the cool of the day. God wants *you* to be a vital, growing member of His family, and He desires to communicate with you and spend time with you—just as a good earthly dad wants to spend time with his children.

Even if nobody else in the entire world wants to have a thing to do with us, our Father wants everything to do with us!

GOD'S DOOR IS ALWAYS OPEN

A number of years ago I was in my office at the church preparing my message notes for the service. I had my door shut so I wouldn't be distracted and could focus my thoughts. All of a sudden, I heard giggling and a *scratchy, scratchy* sound on the door. I looked up to see my four-year-old twin grand-sugars,

Asher and Judah, peeking in through the door with great big smiles, waiting for me to see them. To everyone else my door was shut, but to my sugars, there's never a closed door! I dropped everything and ran to them for my hugs and kisses. At that moment nothing in the world was more important to me than loving and being loved by my sugars!

And it's the same way with God our Father. His door is never shut to us, His "sugars." He'll drop everything when you come and peek in His door. Just like those sugars are the light of my life, we are the lights of God's life. He's just waiting for us to come on in and spend some time with Him! So when you go before Him, express from your heart—and feel in return from His heart—joy, love, peace, pleasure, and acceptance. God our Father's door is always open to you and me.

PEOPLE NEED PEOPLE

Nearly forty years ago the Lord called Larry and me to move to Adelaide, South Australia, and pioneer a church. It was fascinating to see the Lord gather people from every nationality and background together to build a multiracial, multicultural body of believers for Him. We had more than forty-two nationalities in our church and interpreted our services into many different languages. We saw Aussies, Russians, Ukrainians, South Americans, Aboriginals, Tongans, French, Yugoslavs, Hungarians, Mauritians, Fijians, and even a few Americans (our family!) lay aside the barriers of division and build bridges of acceptance, friendship, and love.

In all honesty, this did not come automatically or without resistance. We did everything we possibly could to reach out, befriend, and show kindness to one another. We saw the Lord tear down cultural ideas that historically divided and brought strife in previous years. Larry and I praise God that the impact and relationships from that time period continue to this very day. Not to sound cliché or corny, but love and compassion really can cross all barriers.

During the first several months of building this church, our oldest daughter, Anna, was starting school in Australia. One day a few weeks after she started school, Larry and I heard her in her bedroom, up in the corner of her top bunk bed, crying into her pillow. We rushed in and hugged her and asked what was wrong. Finally, she was able to stop crying enough to tell us that at school the other children were laughing and making fun of her "funny" American accent. She said no one would play with her or talk to her, and at lunch she just sat alone in a corner and ate by herself. During recess, while all the kids ran around, laughed, and played together, she just walked back and forth, back and forth, across the schoolyard, all alone and praying to Jesus.

"BUT JESUS CAN'T PLAY WITH ME"

You can imagine how our hearts broke for our baby girl. In my search for some words that could console her heart, I said, "Anna, even though you feel alone, you're not alone. Jesus is right there with you, inside your heart and walking beside you."

She looked up at me through her tears and said, "I know, Mom, but Jesus can't play with me."

Oh, my! Then we both hugged and sobbed on each other.

There is much to be remembered about this little story. Anna and Larry and I have told this story hundreds of times over the years. It is such a vivid example of the importance and power of the love of God and the love of God's people.

As true as it is that Jesus is always right there with us, it is also true that people need people. That brings me back to mentioning that we should seek to *be* a blessing to others. Let's always try to be conscious of those around us who may need a smile. When you walk into church, especially, ask the Lord to point out someone who needs to be acknowledged, hugged, or encouraged. Sometimes the most spiritual thing we can do is simply be a friend to someone. We are blessed to *be* a blessing to others. Someone said that, as believers, we need to be Jesus with skin on!

Never underestimate God's intervention, help, and

manifestation to our children. As Larry, Anna, and I cried together that day, we shared the love and compassion of a family— mom, dad, and child. Then we shared the love and compassion of God the Father as we prayed together, asking Him to help and bless Anna with His strength and His love for others. We prayed that she would be aware of His presence with her at school. Then we asked Him to intervene and help her make friends and to give her favor at school.

The very next day, she was able to make friends with several little girls, and rather than making fun of her for being American, they wanted to know all about her and America. Prayers answered!

That experience in 1984 was burned into our hearts as parents. We saw God's ability to take care of our family in any circumstance. Anna forever remembers that God loves her and will take care of her (and her own children now) in any circumstance. That foundation of trust in God has been proven over and over again, and even more so in the last several years as we all walked through these health crises together.

We told Anna, "Jesus is right there with you," and He is right there with you too. Whether we are facing the fear of making friends in elementary school, facing the fears of a deadly cancer diagnosis, or facing the fears of the world we all live in right now, Jesus is with us. He loves you, cares about you, and is already working things out in your life.

CHAPTER 9

MY DARKEST DAY
TIZ HUCH

As I'VE BEEN writing this book, my desk is piled high with stacks of my favorite research books, various Bibles, and sermon notes I've taught over the years. There is one stack I've been avoiding—my personal journal notes. I recognize those particular writings from the first few weeks after being diagnosed with aggressive stage 3-C ovarian cancer, having major surgery (a seventeen-inch-long surgery incision), and beginning heavy chemotherapy infusions.

At times I was so sick or sorrowful that I scribbled a few words on a sticky note. Other times I journaled. Frankly, I'm surprised at myself. Before me I see many, many pages of faith declarations of God's Word and promises. Pages and pages of notes offer praise to God for His manifested comfort, hope, and help— small and large miracles and blessings He brought. *Did I really write that?* I did!

While I noted my pain and uncertainties, I can see from my own pen that I always countered my natural experiences with the promises of God. All glory to God for what He did to help me believe His promises as I walked through the everyday affairs of my life!

YOUR ATTITUDE BECOMES YOU

One notebook in particular caught my eye. An orange sticky note is stuck to the top page. At some point I'd jotted down,

"Declaring the Power of God's Promises in Our Thoughts and Words! Your Attitude Becomes You!"

At first I thought I was reading an old message I had put in this file. Then I realized these were not notes I wrote for an old sermon of mine. They were notes I wrote on the darkest day of my life.

It was just a few weeks after my cancer diagnosis. I'd just had major surgery, which removed seven organs. I'd started my first rounds of chemo infusions, which would last for the next six months. I was in physical pain and such an overload and fog that I can barely remember writing all this down.

Even though this reflects the natural side of things, I think it's important that I share them with you. As I said earlier, God can use the natural, medical, and supernatural to bring about our healing. I would like to share my darkest day with you now.

"THIS WAS MY TOUGHEST DAY SO FAR"

August 8, 2019, was the first day that Larry left home without me to film for our TV program, *New Beginnings With Pastors Larry and Tiz Huch*. Larry was incredible and made sure to tell me how much he would miss me and couldn't wait until I could come back and be with him. He assured me that our life would be back to normal again soon. The full weight of not being a part of filming our programs with Larry hit me hard. I felt "left out" from our life. Of course, I wasn't being left out by Larry or anyone else by any means. But in my mind and heart I felt an overwhelming sadness that I was missing out on our life.

I tried to be strong and positive as Larry hugged and kissed me goodbye and left the house alone. I knew it was hard for him too. I went back to bed and broke down and sobbed uncontrollably. In fact, I cried so hard I felt like my seven hundred surgery stitches were going to burst wide open. I had tried to be brave for so long. Now the emotional dam had broken.

As my sobbing lessened, I lay still—barely able to move. I was alone and hollow inside. As I lay there, fearful thoughts and images of what my future may look like came in like a flood to fill the void inside. I was vulnerable and completely exhausted, so the rush of negative thoughts created a whirlpool force, sucking me into it.

This day was not so much about whether God would heal me of cancer. I wasn't thinking about whether I would live or die. This day was about the buildup of emotional turmoil and heaviness that was on me from struggling and dealing with all of this in my mind, emotions, spirit, and body.

During the first several weeks of this crazy trauma, I had been so driven to rise above all the negative reports and hardships that I would not allow these types of negative thoughts and emotions to take control of me. I was bound and determined to "fight the good fight of faith" (1 Tim. 6:12) and stay in a positive mental and spiritual place. But on this day it all came to a head, and I fell apart and let it all out.

Do you know that God can handle our emotional upheavals during crisis? It's true.

LORD, PLEASE HELP ME

Finally, after I had cried all my tears, I mustered up the strength to crawl out of the covers and kneel down on the floor next to my bed. I grabbed my prayer shawl (tallit) and wrapped myself in it, intending to pray.

All I could even get out of my mouth was a little whisper: "Lord, please help me."

With my simple heart's cry, the Holy Spirit came so near, became so real and tangible.

In my heart I started again. "Lord, please help me. I just give all of this to You. I am casting all my cares upon You because I know You love and care for me. I love You and trust You with my life, my family, and my future."

The Tallit: Our Personal Prayer Closet

You may have heard Larry teach on the tallit before. It is a prayer shawl that we are to place over our head and wrap ourselves in to pray. Larry and I do this at certain times of biblical high holidays or at times of great needs. This was definitely a time of great need for me.

The tallit is our private prayer closet we can go in to close out the voices, chaos, circumstances, and chatter of the world around us. We come before God with our needs and receive His supernatural help and miracles. This is exactly what I was doing—on my toughest day so far.

Peace in the Midst of the Storm

I knew I could not just lie in bed and allow myself to be overwhelmed by those negative emotions. God knows me, and He saw this deliberate act of faith.

As I knelt before my God, I could barely whisper, but I knew that He knew. I felt He held me, as a parent would hold their sick or hurting child. No words are necessary to convey love, comfort, or commitment to help. The peace of God filled my heart, mind, and body. He was giving me peace in the midst of my storm.

"Be still, and *know* that I am God."

I heard that scripture (Ps. 46:10, emphasis added) down inside of me, so I took my focus off my fears and put them onto knowing my God and just letting God be God. I shared earlier how it is so important to seek the miracle giver and not just the miracle. This is what I'm talking about. Know your God. Know that He is God. Trust. Be still.

I remember that a deep peace and trust came over me as I heard those words. I can't even really tell you if I fell asleep or what transpired over the next few minutes. Sometime later I took a deep breath. In the silence of my room, the presence of God was with me. Then, still on my knees and under my tallit, I took several deep breaths, held them as long as I could, and exhaled. In my heart I was symbolically breathing in the breath of God. It felt, though, like I was *actually* breathing in the healing breath and life of God! In that moment I realized I felt completely different than I had before I knelt down to pray. The heavy burden had lifted off me. I felt tangibly relieved, lighthearted, soul cleansed, strong, uplifted, and changed.

Instead of a chemotherapy infusion, I felt an infusion of God's peace, hope, faith, strength, confidence, victory, and genuine joy. I got up and felt a need to write down these thoughts on a notepad I kept next to my bed. Then I wrote declarations of faith. Suddenly God's promises bubbled up from within my soul until I was writing promises as fast as they raced through my mind.

Just moments before I was engulfed in raw, emotional despair. God lifted that heaviness and replaced it with His promises and His very real Spirit of hope. We were exchanging my needs for His miracles! It flowed so fast through my mind that my pen could hardly keep up. As I was having my meltdown, He was bringing me my breakthrough! Isaiah 61:3 came alive to me:

> To console those who mourn in Zion, to give them beauty for ashes, the oil of joy for mourning, the garment of praise for the spirit of heaviness; that they may be called trees of righteousness, the planting of the LORD, that He may be glorified.

HIS PROMISES SUSTAINED ME

I knew I still had to walk it all out in the days ahead. But I genuinely had a life-altering, supernatural shift within me, one that I knew would equip me to face all that was ahead of me. God had definitely added His *super* to my *natural*! He met me at my point of need and supernaturally equipped me from the inside out to rise above this.

As I look at these notes from that day and from other pages of God's promises I wrote down in the days that followed, I am amazed at the continual reality of God. Over many years the Holy Spirit had implanted these promises deep within my soul. Now, in my hour of need, I declared them to myself. Now He caused His Word to rise up out of my heart and pen to counter-attack the realities of cancer.

As I said before, I'm not telling these stories to draw attention to myself but to draw attention to our God and bring hope to His people. And I'm not telling them to be dramatic or negative but to be real and open about what we went through. I hope you can relate to this very real struggle and find strength and faith in God's promises as you finish this chapter.

These notes were written as a purposeful act of faith and dominion, not in a time of victory or confidence, or at a high mountaintop peak of faith and accomplishment. These were all written at a time of defeat and despair, at the lowest point of my life, in a deep, dark valley of desperation and fear. Looking back at them, I see each line as a step forward as my mind and heart processed through the steps to victory.

I'm going to share just a few of these declarations with you now, at the end of this chapter. As you read these promises, I hope you will pause to listen to God. Be still and know your God. If God leads you, pick up your pen and jot down a few of your own declarations of His promises to you.

I DECLARE BEFORE GOD...

- I will be positive on purpose.

- I will fill my heart with His presence and His promises, and His peace will come.

- What we dwell on, we become.

- What we focus on, we see.

- What we allow in our mind will stay in until we kick it out and subdue its power and control.

- Our attitude becomes us.

- Our faith becomes us.

- I will guard my heart with all diligence, because out of it flows every issue of my life.

- If my God be for me, who or what can come against me?

- As my days are, so shall my strength be (Deut. 33:25).

- You are the Lord who heals me (Exod. 15:26).

- You will take sickness away from me.

- The number of my days You will fulfill.

- My life and destiny will *not* be cut short from this attack on my health.

- I shall not die, but live and declare Your works (Ps. 118:17).

- God *Himself* is watching over His Word and promise of divine healing and health to perform it in my body (Isa. 55:11).

- My peace is not dependent on my circumstances.

- My future is not dependent on natural circumstances but on God's Word and His miracles.

- My life, health, and future will not be defined by this diagnosis, statistics, or words on the medical reports. It will be defined by God's Word.

- I am not a statistic. I am a child of God and His covenant promises!

- I live by faith, not by sight (Heb. 10:38).

- God is near us when we call on Him from the depths of our heart. He blesses and satisfies His worshippers. He hears our cry and saves us (Ps. 145:18–19).

- Lord, I believe. Help my unbelief (Mark 9:24).

- I choose to magnify my God, *not* my challenges.

- I will not focus on my problems. I will focus on God's promises and power.

- My God is bigger and more powerful than cancer.

- I receive *His* promises above my reports and diagnosis.

- The same Spirit that raised Jesus Christ from the dead lives within us and can bring life to our own lives and bodies (Rom. 8:11).

- I'm not going to be worrying, but I am going to be warring!

- First I choose to believe in faith. Then it begins to flow and become reality within me.

- Put on joy and a smile!

- Sometimes we smile because we're happy. Sometimes we are happy because we smile.

- I choose joy!

- My smile *becomes* me.

- Make the choice to rejoice.

- No matter what circumstances I am facing, through faith I will rise up above them and enter into God's outpouring grace, equipping, strength, favor, peace, joy, anointing, and miracles by the moment.

- I know that God is in control and will see me through it all. He will have the final say.

Amen and amen!

THE AFTERGLOW

After I wrote these declarations (and many more), I put down my pen and paper, raised my hands in praise to the Lord, and thanked Him. I closed my eyes and soaked in His presence, His hope, and His refreshing. I even smiled big toward Him and took a few deep breaths of His Spirit.

Then I got up, dressed, put makeup on, and waited for Larry to come home and tell me all about how the Lord anointed the teachings as he filmed our program.

I pray my story will encourage and inspire you to follow these steps and prayers. May your darkest days become your most precious times enveloped and transformed in the arms and the spirit of the Lord.

CHAPTER 10

WHEN FEAR KNOCKS, PRAY GOD'S PROMISES
Tiz Huch

I ONCE SAW A bumper sticker that said, "Life is fragile. Handle with care!" What good advice. I like to say, "Life is fragile. Handle with *prayer.*" Prayer is not chasing after God and begging Him to help us with our issues in life. Prayer is God's gift to us. God designed prayer to be a two-way communication that helps us to live our daily lives in sync with His will for us.

I want to share with you a cute story about prayer. An old-time little country church needed a new paint job, new carpet, and some sprucing up. There were no extra funds in the church bank account to pay for it. The elders of the church called a special meeting to discuss how to raise funds for the needed projects. Each elder, in turn, offered ideas or suggestions on how to do a fundraiser. One suggested a church garage sale. Others suggested various things nearby churches had done to raise funds.

Finally, the last man folded his arms together and said, "Why don't we gather the whole church and have an old-fashioned prayer meeting and ask God to supply the money we need?"

The room got quiet until one man cried out, "Dear Lord! Has it come to that?"

Kind of funny, but sadly so true. Prayer ought to be our first response, not our last resort! Prayer shouldn't be like a 911 emergency call. Prayer isn't pulling a fire alarm handle when a fire breaks out. Prayer is our lifeline to God.

YOUR NAME IS WRITTEN IN THE PALM OF HIS HAND

It bears repeating—if we want to see God's power move through us, we need to build a relationship with Him. God's power needs faith to activate, and the best way to increase our faith is to know our God and believe His promises in the Bible. When you know God's true nature, it's easy to trust Him. When you read the promises of God, you see that He is a kind, bighearted God. He's not a hard taskmaster. He's not a stingy God. He is a good God—all the time!

When you internalize the truth that God loves you deeply, you will see your future differently. You will see your future through the eyes of God, who has destined you to be successful in the plans He has for you. He's not up there waiting for you to make a mistake so He can kick you when you're down. He is a good and loving Father who is in your corner, cheering for you. What's more, God's abundance is limitless, and He has the means and resources to take care of all your needs and ensure your success.

Simple faith that God loves you will change your life in so many ways. No longer will you be coming to God "begging" Him to have mercy or rescue you. You will understand that it is His own plan out of love for you to change your circumstances for the better. We all battle with low self-esteem and negative thoughts. "Who am I that God Almighty would care about me? I'm not worthy."

We are going to leave those feelings in the dust and in fact buried in the dirt! You are God's precious child. He loves you. He tells us in Isaiah 49:16 that He has our name written on the palm of His hand. When a person commits to getting a tattoo of a loved one on their arm, it symbolizes a commitment and means something deep. God, your Father, has *your* name inscribed on His own hand. That's genuine love and commitment to you!

PRAYER AND FAITH GIVE US ACCESS TO GOD'S UNLIMITED RESOURCES AND MIRACLES

When our family got hit with two separate diagnoses of potentially terminal cancer, the promises of God went to a new level of reality for us. When you are suddenly hanging on a branch on the edge of a cliff peering out over the valley of death below, your prayers and faith aren't a backup plan anymore. They become your lifeline to God's supernatural help and healing. Our faith, prayers, and declarations had to go to an entirely new level.

Even with the most advanced medical solutions, there is still a high risk of losing the battles and no guarantees of success. The highest level of medical doctors will tell you that cancer is a beast with no respect or boundaries. This is why we have been so adamant about connecting God's *super* to our *natural*.

Larry and I have faced down a lot of challenges in forty-five years of marriage and ministry. Together we sought out, carved out, and lived out a life of authentic confidence in God and the promises in His Word. We prayed, preached, and stood in faith for ourselves, our family, and our people and have seen God do incredible miracles time and time again. But never in all our years had we faced battles of this magnitude. We had to "pull out the big guns" on these. This was sink-or-swim time. As Larry has said, "When you're facing a financial crisis, even if you lose everything, there's always some way to recover and rebuild. For the most part, the challenges most of us have faced always have some way out or backup plan. This time everything really is on the line. It's all or nothing."

During our entire ministry, I've taught on the power of prayer and faith. I've always said, "Don't wait until you need a miracle to get to know the miracle worker!" I thank God that before we were hit with these horrific health reports, we had a long history of knowing our God intimately. We had already established a foundation of knowing God's promises and experiencing His power as we pressed in through prayer and perseverance.

Without a doubt, prayer and faith change everything. God's intervention rewrites your future! God's promises are true and "trump" our problems! These are not simply catchy clichés. These are absolute truths that have brought undeniable miracles and breakthroughs to us. He brought us through, and He will bring you through too.

A lot of people quote the verse that says, "The truth will set you free." But it's not just the truth that will set you free; it's the truth you *know* that will set you free. The truth of the Word of God can sit in your Bible on a shelf every day, but that truth doesn't set you free from anything. You can teach a parrot to quote scriptures, but that truth doesn't set anyone free. It is only the truth that we hear, comprehend, and internalize, or "own," that can set us free and change our circumstances and futures. That's why it is critical that we know, receive, and declare the promises of God for our own lives. We have to take ownership of them personally.

BELIEVE IN THE GOD WHO ALREADY BELIEVES IN YOU

When you *know* that God believes in you, it changes the way you feel about yourself and transforms the way you view your life. When you know that God believes in you, your "Goliaths" look smaller. The impossible turns to possible because we know that "with God all things are possible" (Matt. 19:26; Mark 10:27).

When you realize how much God believes in you, it will change the way you view your own potential. You will have hope for your future. Rather than thinking, "Oh, I could never do that," or "That's beyond my abilities," or "My problem is too big even for God to help," you realize that God Almighty lives within you. Because the Spirit of truth dwells within us, we can live beyond the limitations of our own natural talent, ability, IQ, or physical limitation.

We have the opportunity every day to draw from the well of God's Spirit and the living Word within us and tap directly into the mind and resources of God Himself! The very God who spoke and formed the world lives within you and me. The moment we asked Him into our hearts and were born-again, His Spirit took up residence and started living within us.

One of my favorite Scripture passages has always been Ephesians 3:16–20:

> ...That He would grant you, according to the riches of His glory, to be strengthened with might through His Spirit in the inner man, that Christ may dwell in your hearts through faith; that you, being rooted and grounded in love, may be able to comprehend with all the saints what is the width and length and depth and height—to know the love of Christ which passes knowledge; that you may be filled with all the fullness of God. Now to Him who is able to do exceedingly abundantly above all that we ask or think, according to the power that works in us.

Paul was talking about being strengthened with might by God's Spirit in our inner man. So we see here that God's power is already alive and working within us, for us, and through us.

THE SAME SPIRIT THAT RAISED JESUS FROM THE DEAD IS IN ME

Romans 8:11 says, "The Spirit of him who raised Jesus from the dead is living in [us]" and "will also give life to [our] mortal bodies through his Spirit, who lives in [us]" (NIV). Do you grasp the significance of that? The same Spirit who raised Jesus from the dead and brought Him back to life is living within us. That same Spirit can raise us up and enable us to do whatever He has put within our hearts to do!

This scripture has always had deep meaning for me and the people I pray for, no matter the circumstance. However, going through these past few years of fighting cancer for Lion and then myself, this scripture took on an entirely new reality. Every single day and night I prayed and boldly declared this scripture over

Lion and myself. No matter how sad, sick, weak, or hopeless I felt in the natural, I made a point to speak this scripture (and many others) out loud as a declaration of faith and dominion. There is genuine creative power within our faith and spoken words that connects God's *super* to our *natural*. When we boldly declare God's promises, three things happen to release the miraculous power of God:

1. We *declare to God* our faith and trust in Him, His Word, and His promises.

2. We *declare to the enemy* and our circumstances that they have no dominion over our health, finances, family, or future.

3. We *release the creative supernatural power* and dominion of God's spoken Word into our lives, minds, bodies, and circumstances.

God's Word is a *living* Word. It is a seed that holds His supernatural power to grow and reproduce and bear fruit within you.

The same resurrection power that raised Jesus from the dead can raise you up from any kind of attack of the world. Our God can break every chain, every bondage, every spirit of limitation or containment, every addiction, every emotional problem or stronghold, every sickness, every disease, and every form of oppression or attack that tries to hold you captive. The name of Jesus is above every other name, report, or force.

We read in Daniel 11:32, "The people who know their God shall be strong, and carry out great exploits." *The people who know their God*—that's you and me. Those of us who *know* our God and His promises will be strong and do world-shaking exploits! Those exploits will shake your own life and even the entire world. It's time that God's people live in the full and complete power of the resurrection.

Larry and I love to teach about God's promises and pray for people. But do you know what's better than that? We love to see people grasp the revelation and walk on their own in faith and miracles. When you plant the seed of God's Word in your mind, soul, and body, it begins to grow and reproduce itself within you.

Invite God's Spirit to dwell in your heart. Pour the thirst-quenching water of God's promises into your spirit. Then pull up the bucket from the well in your soul. That's where God is living. He's not way out there in the dark, distant universe somewhere. His very Spirit is living inside you. You have the ability to call and draw upon His help, His strength, His healing, His wisdom, His resources and provisions, His creativity, His intelligence, His passion, His anointing—whatever you need, it's right there within you. Isn't that exciting? The fact that God Almighty lives and reigns within you and me is pretty amazing, isn't it? What an incredible honor we have as the children of God!

PRAYER ACTIVATES THE PROMISES OF GOD

You might be wondering, "If God loves me and knows what I'm going through, why doesn't He just do something about it?" The blessings we're promised are not necessarily automatic. We have to ask for, believe for, and activate God's promises through prayer.

The Bible assures us over and over that the Lord sees and knows about all our needs. Matthew 6:8, for example, says, "Your Father knoweth what things ye have need of, before ye ask him" (KJV). But we still have to ask in faith to move His hand.

Let me give you an illustration. This process is similar to what happens when you receive a new credit card in the mail. You are given the card with full authorization and backing, but you still need to make a phone call to activate it before using the card to make any purchases. In like fashion, God has sent His Word with full authorization and backing, but we still have to make the call of prayer and faith to activate it. We have to ask! There is God's part, and there is our part.

The Gospel of John confirms this idea. In John 14:12–14, Jesus said, "Truly, truly, I say to you, he who believes in Me, the works that I do, he will do also; and greater works than these he will do; because I go to the Father. Whatever you ask in My name, that will I do, so that the Father may be glorified in the Son. If you ask Me anything in My name, I will do it" (NASB).

The Lord never intended for His children to live within the confines and limitations of this natural world. His plan has always been to empower and equip us with His supernatural blessings—to add His *super* to our *natural*. When we do our best, He will do the rest. But we have to ask!

WE LIVE IN A FALLEN WORLD

When Larry and I were first coming to terms with the attacks on our family's health, we had a chance to have lunch with our longtime friends and highly respected ministers Rabbi Daniel and Susan Lapin. We were drawing deep upon their wisdom, knowledge of the Word of God, experiences, and compassion.

Larry asked them, "In your opinion, why do things like this happen? Why doesn't God just intervene and circumvent these things?"

Rabbi Lapin said, "We live in a fallen, broken world. If God just circumvented bad things in the lives of all His people, we would never even realize His help or intervention. It is in our need for His help that He is able to co-labor with us and show Himself strong on our behalf. It is also a way He demonstrates His love and miraculous power to the world. It is a beautiful gift that God would choose to co-labor with us, His children, to repair the broken world and even our own broken hearts and worlds. To some degree we will experience the effects of that on our own lives. The Word tells us that the rain will fall on the just and the unjust. So even though we are righteous, just, and God's children, the rain and fallout of a fallen, broken world will impact us too."

Rabbi Lapin explained that living in a fallen world adds to the causes of the challenges we face in our lives. We live in a broken world, in need of repair. We are given the task to *tikkun olam*, a Hebrew term that means to "repair a broken world."

Rabbi Lapin said, "Because you and Tiz are still so aggressively pursuing changing the world, [or] *tikkun olam*—repairing this broken world—we are confident that God will heal and restore Tiz and Lion and your family. If you were retiring, scaling back your vision and purpose for your ministry, things might look different. You two still have a lot of work to do for God and in repairing the world. Your best days are not behind you. Your best days are ahead of you! You two are just getting started!"

As we prayed together, our hearts were knit into a deeper bond. Tears fell as God's presence touched us and filled our hearts with hope and courage for the days ahead.

A WORD TO THE WEARY

We all can get the wind knocked out of us. We live in a fallen world, and we certainly can grow weary on our journeys.

Maybe you are feeling discouraged, weary, or brokenhearted. Maybe you're wondering why you're going through something or why God didn't just intervene or circumvent these things. Remember the words of Rabbi Lapin. We live in a fallen, broken world. If God just circumvented bad things in the lives of all His people, we would never even realize His help or intervention. When we need God's help, He co-labors with us and shows Himself strong on our behalf. Our Lord wants to demonstrate His love and miraculous power to us and to the world.

Our God heals broken hearts, repairs broken relationships, and heals broken bodies. He sees you, cares about you, and is able to change your life for the better. Rise up, as Larry and I did that day, determined to lay hold of God's miracles and His destiny for your life!

JESUS IS PASSING BY—SEIZE YOUR OPPORTUNITY

The tenth chapter of Mark tells us the story of Bartimaeus, a blind beggar from Jericho. He sat by the roadside, day after day, appealing to the sympathies of passersby.

One day was different, however—Jesus came to Jericho. As He and His disciples were leaving the city, they passed by blind Bartimaeus, who shouted out, "Jesus, thou son of David, have mercy on me" (Mark 10:47, KJV).

Other people around Bartimaeus urged him to be quiet, but he shouted even more loudly, "Thou son of David, have mercy on me" (v. 48, KJV).

Because of the beggar's persistence, Jesus called Bartimaeus to Him and inquired, "What do you want Me to do for you?" (See verse 51.)

Bartimaeus answered, "Lord, that I might receive my sight" (v. 51, KJV).

The Bible says he immediately received his sight, and Jesus Himself explained why. He told Bartimaeus, "Go thy way; thy *faith* hath made thee whole" (v. 52, KJV, emphasis added).

Bartimaeus was healed because he seized his opportunity and cried out, "Jesus! Don't pass me by! This is my moment. Heal my blind eyes!" The Bible records that Jesus heard his cry, stopped, saw his faith, granted his request, and healed him. How many other blind men did *not* cry out to Jesus and grab ahold of His promises by faith—and therefore missed out on their healing?

This account is an excellent example of how the spiritual realm operates. God knows our needs and sees our issues, but He can respond only to our faith and prayers. Let's never be guilty of letting Jesus pass us by and miss an opportunity for our miracle. Jesus is passing by—let's seize our opportunity! Are you ready to do as blind Bartimaeus did and lay hold of the miracles the Lord has for you? I know you are!

Pray With Me

Let's pray in agreement together right now. Read this prayer out loud as you pray to Him:

> *Father God, I come before You today in faith and prayer. Thank You that You love me, care for me, and see me and the things I'm going through. I give my life, heart, and circumstances to You. I cast my cares and anxieties upon You because You care for me (1 Pet. 5:7). I let go of my struggles, weariness, and discouragement. I lay hold of Your promises, blessings, and miracles to change the course of my life. I reach out in faith and seize my opportunity to rise up out of my circumstances and receive my miracles right now. Thank You that, from this moment forward, my heart, body, and life are no longer broken. I know that Your outpouring of restoration and miracles is being released in me, and my greatest days are ahead of me. The best is yet to come! Amen.*

Now give God thanks and praise for what He has done for you!

CHAPTER 11

THE ANOINTING
OF THE HOLY SPIRIT
FOR YOU AND ME

Tiz Huch

I N MINISTRY, THE experience of the *anointing* is eagerly sought after. The *anointing* is referred to as the tangible presence and power of the Holy Spirit in a church service, prayer meeting, or circumstance.

The anointing of God is not just so that we can get Holy Ghost goose bumps and excitement. That's fine, but the anointing of God is tangible, and God sends His anointing to set us free and to bring glory to God!

GOD'S REALITY AT THE POINT OF OUR NEEDS

When Jesus was on the earth, He entered a synagogue and walked up front to read from the scrolls. He turned to Isaiah 61 and read a portion of this chapter out loud. Then He announced, "Today this scripture has been fulfilled in your hearing."

It's true. Jesus was sent by God to provide for us His divine exchange—all our darkness for all His love and light. Isaiah 61:1–3 is one of my all-time favorite scriptures. Let's read His promises now in this passage:

The Spirit of the LORD GOD is upon Me, because the LORD has anointed Me to preach good tidings to the poor; He has sent Me to heal the brokenhearted, to proclaim liberty to the captives, and the opening of the prison to those who are bound; to proclaim the acceptable year of the LORD, and the day of vengeance of our God; to comfort all who mourn, to console those who mourn in Zion, to give them beauty for ashes, the oil of joy for mourning, the garment of praise for the spirit of heaviness; that they may be called trees of righteousness, the planting of the LORD, that He may be glorified.

I think every one of us can relate to the example and understanding of "ashes," "mourning," and "heaviness" spoken of in Isaiah 61:3. But do we understand how to receive the genuine exchange of our ashes for His beauty, our mourning for His oil of joy, and our spirit of heaviness for His garment of praise?

I believe Jesus' words that day are still relevant to me and you, right now in the world we live in. Yes, eternity is real and will be wonderful beyond our wildest imaginations. Yes, things will ease up and get better over the course of time. But God's intentions for His people are to equip us, turn evil into good, heal us, bless us, and fill us. Jesus' anointing flows over us now that we are born-again and we walk in His abilities. With our Lord's anointing, we will see change in our circumstances and experience His supernatural flow of miracles by the moment.

GOOD NEWS FOR BAD TIMES

The Bible is good news for bad times. God's precious anointing can come alive to us as we read the pages of His Word. The Bible brings hope where there is no hope. But, above all, the Bible tells us what God wants to do supernaturally when we call upon Him in prayer and faith. The Bible paints the picture of who God is and the reality of His existence in the world and in our individual lives.

We can tend to think of scriptures as though they're a nice

saying on a greeting card or verses to a song. Nice, sweet, but not meant to be taken literally. What did these words and phrases actually mean at the time they were written? What do they mean in real time in our real lives and world as we face real issues?

Of course, there is great historical context of the time this scripture was written by the prophet Isaiah. But I believe there is truth here for you and me right now.

BEAUTY FOR ASHES

In ancient biblical times in Israel, ashes exemplified loss and mourning. Believe it or not, if you were grieving the death of a loved one, the custom was to actually sit in ashes and sprinkle yourself with ashes. Sometimes people did this after a personal tragedy or a national disaster.

Although this particular expression of grief is foreign to us, we can all relate to the feeling of losing someone special to us. In biblical times, ashes were a representation of those feelings of loss, deep sadness, or yearning for what once was. In the natural, ashes are the physical debris left over after things are burned up in flames. Ashes are left after something is destroyed forever. The customs and expressions of grief have changed since Bible times, but the emotional upheaval is the same. I wonder if this might be where the modern term *burned-out* came from.

The COVID-19 pandemic, and then its variants such as Omicron, Delta, and so on, have been unending. People experienced hardships on every level of life, from death of loved ones to illness to loss of jobs to financial hardships and social isolation. These "flames of fire" swept across the world and left piles of ashes in place of what was once normal life. Burned-out could well describe the feelings of many people as we continue to hope that this virus will wind down and cease altogether. For the Huch family, our last few years also included battles against cancer, battles that left us feeling burned-out too.

And God brings us His divine exchange—His beauty to replace our ashes! Praise God! This is truly what the Lord has done for our own family. Out of the ashes of our fiery trial there arose beautiful new beginnings. God has multiplied a beautiful life to restore what the enemy tried to steal. He can do the same for you!

OIL OF JOY FOR MOURNING

We know that oil is always used as a symbol of the Holy Spirit. Oil represents the release of God's anointing—to "smear," or cover and fill, us with His equipping and abilities and empower us with His authority and dominion.

When the depths of grief and mourning are so deep within our souls, it seems that nothing can touch that place of deep pain and suffering. The oil of joy is an image of God's loving, healing Spirit running even deeper into our souls than the pain of mourning. God's oil of joy cradles and comforts our mourning heart. When our Father applies His oil to His broken-hearted child, healing begins and the heart is stirred to believe that wholeness is possible.

In the natural realm of life, oil impacts many areas of our lives. Think about it. We use oil in our car engines, bicycle chains, squeaky door hinges, and on and on. Good old WD-40 is a staple in every household, garage, and barn. Why? Because oil penetrates deeply and does things that nothing else can do. It oozes deep into cracks, crevices, and damaged parts. It cleanses, loosens built-up gunk and debris, lubricates seized-up parts, softens dry parts, protects from further damage, renews, cools down, loosens tension, protects, smooths out rough edges, soothes worn-out surfaces, and causes chains that are rusty and locked up to move smoothly and unencumbered.

Picture your own hands after a day of working in the garden or a dusty shop, barn, or garage as they are parched, dry, and cracked. Nothing feels better than rubbing them with soothing, enriching oils or creams.

Now take all these examples and apply them to your parched, ragged, damaged, seized-up, encumbered, weary, and broken heart. God's oil of joy for mourning can do the same thing, only in the emotional and spiritual realms of your heart and soul.

Corrie ten Boom was a survivor of the horrors of the Holocaust in a Nazi concentration camp during World War II. After the war Corrie traveled all over the world to testify of God's love. In one particular meeting she spoke about God's forgiveness. To her surprise, one of the meanest prison guards from Ravensbrück walked down the aisle after the meeting, extended his hand, and asked Corrie to forgive him.

At first Corrie could not move her hand to meet his. She wondered if saying, "I forgive you," could erase her sister's death in that horrible prison camp. What about all the women this man beat and threw into the gas chambers? Corrie prayed and asked God for His help to forgive. As she did, she said she felt the tangible anointing of God go down her arm as she lifted it.

Corrie shook the former guard's hand and said, "I forgive you, brother."

Corrie famously stated, "There is no pit so deep God's love is not deeper still."[1]

God will give you the grace to forgive people who hurt you. No matter the circumstances or how deep the personal pit of grief is, God's love and grace are deeper still. He is not only with us in the fire, but He is able to take away our grief and exchange our sorrows for His supernatural joy.

A GARMENT OF PRAISE FOR THE SPIRIT OF HEAVINESS

Later in this book I will talk about the power of prayer and teach you more in-depth about spiritual warfare. There are times, though, when we just need to wrap ourselves in a warm blanket of God's love, promises, and presence. It's like coming inside from the cold rain or snow and wrapping yourself in a blanket that's been warming in front of an open fire. It's like putting on a warm garment to chase away the bone-chilling cold.

Some of my heaviest times on this journey were on Sundays.

Larry and I have been doing life together—as one—for over forty-five years. Every Sunday we get ready together, drive to church together, pray together, and preach, teach, and pray for people together. We drive home together and talk about the message and the miracles and highlight how the Lord blessed our church that day. We rejoice in the "fruit of our labor[s]" together (Ps. 128:2, NIV).

The first few months after my surgery and then chemo, I was too weak or sickly to go to church. I missed staff meetings, church events, and interacting with the people of God.

Throughout the pandemic, I had to stay quarantined quite a lot because my immune system was compromised and I was vulnerable to infectious diseases.

Sunday mornings hit me hard. I'd send Larry off to church with kisses and hugs and declare, "Give 'em heaven! And tell everyone hi for me!" I'd pour him his mug of coffee to go, wave goodbye to him, and smile as he pulled out of the garage. Then I'd close the door and lose it.

I felt so sad for Larry because I knew how hard it was for him to go by himself and how alone he felt without me. And I felt so alone and isolated from all that our life revolves around. Of course, the heaviness, darkness, and fears of what the future might hold lurked in the back of my mind. I knew the Lord was the answer to cancer. I was doing my absolute best to be strong and optimistic. In the meantime, I still had to walk out the ongoing real issues in real life in real time.

BEING BRUTALLY HONEST

After Larry left for church, I cleaned up, dressed, tidied the house, and got ready for "Stream Church." We livestream every service so people from all over the world can join us by the internet. It feels like you're right there in the service from the worship singing and the message to the altar call and closing. I'm thankful we have such an incredible technological way to connect people from nearly anywhere on earth. For me, it was the next best thing to being there in person—except I *wasn't* there in person.

As I watched the livestream, the main camera shot of the platform was from the back of the sanctuary, which of course showed my empty seat front and center as the service went on without me. This broke my heart.

I watched our son-in-law, Brandin, lead our church into praise and worship and into the presence of the Holy Spirit. I saw the close-up camera shots of my kids in their seats on the front row praising God and pressing into His presence with their hands high in the air, singing and worshipping from their hearts and mouths, sometimes with tears streaming down their faces. I knew how hard it was on them that all this was going on and that I wasn't there too. If you didn't know the behind-the-scenes story, you would never know, by the looks on their faces, that they were going through such traumatizing times themselves. I sobbed my way through worship.

After singing, Larry would take the service, greet everyone, then tell the congregation to turn to the camera and "wave and say hi to Tiz." As they all did, my heart would be touched, and more tears would flow. Then Larry would preach his message and pray for people, and I'd cry some more.

Let me add that I knew how hard it was for Larry to carry on without me and that he himself was processing. Sometimes he would choke up during the service. Other times he filmed our television program without me, and he'd choke up as he updated our congregation, TV partners, and stream family about how I was doing. But an incredible infilling of God's grace and anointing enabled him to rise up above all this and continue to bring the Word, encouragement, and hope to other people's lives.

SAD SUNDAYS

My sad Sundays were compounded by the fact that I would sit at my desk in my home office and watch the livestream service on my computer screen. It was impossible to ignore the reflection of myself with my bald head, sunken eyes, sallow complexion, puffy face, and no eyelashes or eyebrows, sobbing. As hard as I tried to focus on and participate in the worship, I was overwhelmed by the emotions all these stark images in front of me stirred up. It was like an out-of-body experience. There I sat in front of my computer screen watching my normal life—except without me in it. Life was carrying on without me.

This probably sounds overdramatic, but when you are suddenly facing down the reality of aggressive stage 3 ovarian cancer, your entire perspective on life (in the natural realm) is colored by the very real possibility of not surviving this—short term or long term.

I am being brutally honest about the battles in our minds and how to face them down and overcome them. The battle is real. The reports are real. The cancer is real. But, above all that, our God is real! His promises are real! His miracles are real!

HOW I OVERCAME THE SPIRIT OF HEAVINESS

I will say over and over throughout this book that faith is not turning a blind eye to the challenges we face. But faith is absolutely denying that natural reality the right to rule and reign in our future.

Now, let me tell you how I overcame this spirit of heaviness.

After a few Sundays of this same pattern, I realized I couldn't let Sunday mornings be my private times of falling apart. Sunday morning services needed to be my own private refueling, uplifting, inspirational times of supernatural touches from God again. I had to focus not on what I was missing but on what I was receiving. I had allowed myself to watch the services as a spectator rather than a participant and receiver. I allowed my negative feelings and emotions to override my spiritual connection to the Lord and the infilling of the Holy Spirit. So I changed my game plan and took steps to refocus.

DELIBERATE STEPS TO REFOCUS ON
THE LORD ON SAD SUNDAYS

The first thing I did was move from my office desktop computer to my laptop computer on our kitchen counter and position the laptop so I could not see my own reflection on the screen. I had to get the focus on myself out of my vision. Standing in faith sometimes takes deliberate measures not to see yourself as you currently are but to see yourself as you are believing to become.

The second thing I did to refocus on Sundays was to dress nicely, put on makeup, and carry myself as if I were actually going to church. I didn't wear dressy church clothes, but not frumpy sweats either. Then I put on one of my ball caps to cover my bald head. I always feel better when I look better. I seriously needed to see my new self to come.

The third thing I did was put a guard on my heart. I determined that I would not fall into the dark emotions, not focus on what I was missing out on, but focus in on my own personal time and presence with the Lord. I created within myself an emotional atmosphere of faith and the confident expectation of God's supernatural presence.

The fourth thing I did was carry myself as I do in church as a leader, minister, and woman of God. I am always very deliberate about bringing a joyful, excited, and uplifted spirit into our church services. Rather than dragging through the house tired, discouraged, and downcast, I purposely straightened myself up and acted as if I was already on the other side of my miracle healing.

The fifth thing I did was lift my head and *smile*. John 16:20 says, "Your sorrow will be turned into joy." Larry and I live this way and have taught it for years. Acts 13:52 says that the Lord's disciples were filled with joy and the Holy Spirit. Larry and I had developed the habit of joy in the past, and I was bound and determined to do it even under these circumstances. The Lord is the lifter of my head, but I've learned not to sit around and wait for God to lift my head. I'm going to prime the pump and speed up the process by lifting my own head and heart in faith to Him and allow Him to pour in the real substance of healing and joy. Philippians 4:4 tells us, "Rejoice in the Lord always. *Again* I say rejoice" (emphasis added). I call this the choice to rejoice. Simply put, no matter what is going on, choose to focus on whatever is true, good, praiseworthy, and of a good report. When we deliberately do this, the peace of God, which transcends all negative circumstances, will fill our hearts, minds, and souls. This scripture is one of my favorites and a go-to for my life. No matter what is going on around me or within me, I have the power to rise above it by the choice to rejoice. If I can convey this one key to people, I guarantee you dynamic change will follow.

The sixth thing I did was symbolically put on the garment of praise for the spirit of heaviness. In the natural realm I was feeling tired, weary, and heavy-laden. I deliberately "put on" praise, worship, thankfulness, joy, and declarations of magnifying God. By faith I was entering into a divine exchange of

- my weakness for His strength,

- my sickness for His healing,

- my sadness for His joy, and

- my limitations for His unlimited miracles by the moment.

The seventh thing I did was magnify the Lord in my praise, my faith declarations, and my mind's perspective. Psalm 69:30 says, "I will praise the name of God with a song, and will magnify Him with thanksgiving." In the natural realm, when you look through a magnifying glass at something, what happens? What you look at becomes larger, focused, clearer, and dominant. Right? Our choices to praise and magnify God become the conduit that connects us to God Himself and His supernatural help. There's a powerful business axiom that says, "What we focus on determines what we see. It also determines what we miss." We have the opportunity to either magnify God and His promises or magnify our challenges. Let's make a habit of focusing on and magnifying God, His promises, and His power!

The eighth thing I did was always have my Bible, notebook, and pen with me to take notes and receive revelation from the Lord during Larry's messages—just as I normally do in church. Listen, when I come to church, I am coming to hear, learn, and receive a touch from God. My Bible is packed full of my hand-written notes, revelations, declarations, testimonies, and miracles that God has done for us. It is not just words on pages. It is the living Word of God that comes out of those pages and into the reality of our lives. My focus on Sundays in my kitchen at home was the same as it is in my seat on the front row at church. I was ready, expectant, and determined to hear from God and be transformed in His presence.

GLAD SUNDAYS

As the livestream service began in worship, I stood, just as I do in church, and seriously began singing and praising God. I pressed into God's presence and anointing—watching the stream not as a spectator this time but as a participant. Again, I saw my family on the front row, Brandin leading worship, and my empty seat, but I refused to let my emotions get pulled into the sorrow of not being there with them.

Rather than focusing on my own needs and issues, I looked at the camera shots of the people in our congregation as they lifted their voices and hands in praise, pressing in for the needs in their own lives. My focus shifted off myself and onto the precious people that God had placed under our shepherding care. Rather than being overwhelmed with sadness, despair, and grief, my heart became overwhelmed with gratitude, love, and compassion for them and their families. I saw people I know and some that I haven't met yet, contending for the move of God in their own lives, some with tears streaming down their cheeks. Tears began to stream down my own face, but not for myself or my family—this time for our people. My tears and prayers were not for God to move for me but for God to move for them. A deep passion rose within me to push through this attack on my health and get back to our normal life and calling—not for my sake, but for our people's sake.

I remember feeling so moved by the privilege of being a part of God touching people's lives that I cried tears of joy. A love and deep desire burned within me. I wanted to do more for God!

As I attended New Beginnings Stream Service that day, not as a pastor but as a woman, wife, mom, and nana, our heavenly Father met me at the point of my need and filled me to overflowing with His Spirit. Believe me, I'm not trying to sound dramatic, religious, or super spiritual.

On that Sunday, I can only say that Isaiah 61:1–3 came out of the pages of my Bible and into the reality of my life. The scripture I had declared and prayed for others thousands of times manifested into my personal being that day and ever since. Jesus stood in the synagogue, read this scripture from the Torah scroll, and declared that the Spirit and anointing of God was upon Him and that the scripture was fulfilled in their hearing. Read this passage with me now, from the perspective of my teaching and experiences and in relation to your own life and needs. Read it slowly and let it sink in deeply. Take ownership of this promise, insert your own name in place of "they" and "those," and let the Holy Spirit touch you and speak to you personally.

> The Spirit of the Sovereign LORD is on me, because the LORD has anointed me to proclaim good news to the poor. He has sent me to bind up the brokenhearted, to proclaim freedom for the captives and release from darkness for the prisoners, to proclaim the year of the LORD's favor and the day of vengeance of our God, to comfort all who mourn, and provide for those who grieve in Zion—to bestow on them a crown of beauty instead of ashes, the oil of joy instead of mourning, and a garment of praise instead of a spirit of despair. They

will be called oaks of righteousness, a planting of the
LORD for the display of his splendor.

—ISAIAH 61:1–3, NIV

Just now, writing this and reading it out loud myself, I am
rushing with the anointing of the Holy Spirit! Those goose
bumps, or "Holy Ghost bumps," are real. I pray you are feeling
this too and experiencing the reality of the presence and power
of the Lord!

THE GARMENT OF PRAISE

In all we went through with Lion and then my own diagnosis, I
can honestly tell you that these were the darkest times we have
ever experienced as a family. I can also tell you that we have experienced the realities of these scriptures in our journeys through
the past few years. Words can't begin to explain the supernatural grace of God that lifted me and my family and carried us
through all these painful times. My deepest, darkest times were
also my sweetest and most real times of experiencing the reality
of God's presence, grace, and love. The words in Isaiah 61:3 of
God giving us "beauty for ashes, the oil of joy for mourning,
[and] the garment of praise for the spirit of heaviness" illustrate
these genuine feelings and experiences with Him.

In addition to my heart and soul being healed that day, I was
healed physically. I had been experiencing severe pain in my
abdomen from the surgery. The incision was seventeen inches
long, and the oncologist had removed several organs. Obviously,
I needed some recovery time and dealt with pain issues.

As I worshipped by livestream that day, I placed my hands on
my stomach, declared God's supernatural healing over this surgery incision pain, and prayed for expedient recovery. I claimed
Psalm 103 (as I do every day), that He would renew my youth
as the eagle's. As the streaming service ended, I felt the Spirit
of God so strong that I lifted my hands in praise and thanksgiving for who He is and all He does. Suddenly, I realized that

the sharp pain was gone from my abdomen. I moved around and bent over a few times to be sure, but it definitely was gone and never returned!

Truly, God showered me with another layer of miracles by the moment that day and in the days and months to follow. To reduce my story to one giant miracle healing would be an understatement and an injustice to all the continual miracles that God did. Big or small, God covered them all!

There have been thousands of tangible, progressive healings, not just of my body but of my heart and soul. The reason for the title of this book, *Miracles by the Moment*, is because that phrase became our motto during these journeys. One giant miracle the day after our diagnosis would have been very dynamic and greatly welcomed. The saying "one and done" could have been the name of this book. And it could have been a thirty-page booklet rather than a long, extensive manuscript!

However, as it unfolded and turned out, miracles by the moment is how we got through, overcame, and survived cancer and leukemia. We will share as we go some of the miracles that stand out in addition to the obvious big ones of Lion and me being completely healed and cancer-free. May our stories of God's miracles by the moment encourage and bring hope to you for the journey and healing of your own heart, soul, mind, and body.

My prayer for you is that God will shine as bright in your experiences as He has for me and my family in ours. Trust Him, press into His presence, magnify Him, take Him at His Word, and let God be God!

CHAPTER 12

THE NAMES OF GOD REVEAL THE NATURE OF GOD
TIZ HUCH

WHAT'S IN A name? Today, in our culture, people don't think much about what a name means. In times past, most last names were related to the profession of the person. For instance, the surname *Taylor* may be traced back to an ancestor who was actually a tailor.

In an even greater way, the names of God actually express who He is and who He wants to be in our lives. One of the greatest ways to know God is to know His names. If we want to know God, then we will be eager to discover how He identifies Himself. There is a progression that happens as we study the meaning of God's names:

1. Our foundations of faith, hope, and confidence grow.

2. Our relationship with the Lord deepens.

3. His blessings and miracles flow more freely and frequently.

4. Our prayers and faith explode in power with the realities of who God is and wants to be in our lives.

5. Rather than coming to God begging Him to help us, we boldly receive and enter into who He already is and what He has already done for us.

Let's look at just a few of the names of God as revealed in His Word:

- Jehovah Tsidkenu: The God who is our righteousness
- Jehovah Mekoddishkem: The God who sanctifies us
- Jehovah Shalom: The God who fills us with His peace
- Jehovah Rohi: The God who is our shepherd and guide
- Jehovah Jireh: The God who provides
- El Shaddai: The God of more than enough
- Jehovah Rapha: The God who heals us
- El Roi: The God who sees me
- Jehovah Nissi: The Lord is my banner of victory
- Jehovah Tsuri: God is my rock
- Jehovah Sabaoth: The Lord of hosts
- El Olam: The eternal God
- Jehovah Shammah: The God who is there
- Immanuel: God is with us

Notice that every one of God's names relates to His love and commitment to His people. The names of God do not express some intangible power "out there" in the universe. The names of God carry substance. These names express God's longing and ability to take care of us. Our God never intended His people to try to get by on their own. From the beginning, God's longing has been for *you*. He wants to know you, and He wants you to know Him. He desires continual interactions with those who love Him and have chosen Him. He is the same yesterday, today, and forever.

Let's take a closer look at the names of God I mentioned above so you will know how each one of God's names relates to you and your life.

JEHOVAH TSIDKENU: THE GOD WHO IS OUR RIGHTEOUSNESS

We all deal with feelings of low self-esteem. When was the last time you thought, "I'm not good enough to do that"? Many of us struggle with thoughts that we are not good enough, righteous enough, holy enough, or worthy enough for God to accept us or help us.

As human beings, we do fall short. Romans 3:23 says, "For all have sinned and fall short of the glory of God." But we need to realize that when we receive Jesus' forgiveness and invite His Holy Spirit to live inside us, His righteousness becomes our righteousness. Second Corinthians 5:21 says that Jesus became sin for us "that we might become the righteousness of God in Him."

Jehovah Tsidkenu—what a name! What a promise!

JEHOVAH MEKODDISHKEM: THE GOD WHO SANCTIFIES US

To be sanctified means to be set apart *from* sin and death and set apart *to* God and eternal life. When we are born-again, He adopts us to be His very own child.

> Christ also loved the church and gave Himself for her, that He might sanctify and cleanse her with the washing of water by the word, that He might present her to Himself a glorious church, not having spot or wrinkle or any such thing, but that she should be holy and without blemish.
>
> —EPHESIANS 5:25–27

Our God sanctifies us and sets us apart for His own purposes and destiny! Only God can cleanse us and make us holy and unblemished for Himself. It is not our own righteousness or perfection that qualifies us for His acceptance and blessings. It is His love, mercy, and grace that qualify us and set us apart for all He has for us.

JEHOVAH SHALOM: THE GOD WHO FILLS US WITH HIS PEACE

Shalom is the Hebrew word for peace, wholeness, harmony, and completeness. Shalom peace is not dependent on circumstances. True and deep peace comes as we trust in the Lord in all areas of our lives regardless of the circumstances, highs and lows, and ups and downs.

In John 14:27, Jesus said, "Peace I leave with you, My peace I give to you; not as the world gives do I give to you. Let not your heart be troubled, neither let it be afraid."

When we are fearful, the Holy Spirit brings us peace. No matter what our surrounding circumstances are, the Holy Spirit can fill us and refill us with God's supernatural peace.

JEHOVAH ROHI: THE GOD WHO IS OUR SHEPHERD AND GUIDE

One of the most familiar of all Bible passages is Psalm 23:1, which says, "The Lord is my shepherd. I shall not want." This means that we will not "want for," or be in need of, any good thing. Our Lord is good, and He will lead us and put light on our pathway so we can see, even when all else is dark around us.

Our Shepherd leads us step-by-step. However, from His perspective He sees our lives from above, from the beginning to the end. He goes before us to set things up and lead us into our destinies. Nothing that happens in our lives takes Him by surprise. Before we ever even have a hint of a problem, He has already gone ahead and worked out the answers, provisions, and miracles for us. When the Lord is our Shepherd, we can believe for His miracles, moment by moment.

JEHOVAH JIREH: THE GOD WHO PROVIDES

God gave His people a covenant of blessing, as explained in Deuteronomy 28:1–14. Here are some of the covenant blessings that are yours if you obey the Lord your God and are careful to observe His commandments:

- blessed in the city

- blessed in the country

- blessed in the fruit of your body

- blessed in the produce of your ground

- blessed in the increase of your herds, your cattle, and your flocks

- blessed in your basket and your kneading bowl (daily bread)

- blessed when you come in

- blessed when you go out

- blessed in your storehouses

- blessed in all you set your hand to do

- blessed in the land the Lord gives you

- your enemies who rise against you shall be defeated

- your enemy will come against you one way and flee before you seven ways

And that's not all. Verse 13 says, "And the Lord will make you the head and not the tail; you shall be above only, and not be beneath, if you heed the commandments of the Lord your God, which I command you today, and are careful to observe them."

Our Jehovah Jireh desires to bless us and bring us into a good land with plentiful provisions. It is His will to bless and multiply everything we put our hands to do.

The Bible gives us hundreds of scriptures telling us of God's financial blessings. He is absolutely not against us having things. He is against things having us, though. When we honor Him, He will honor us.

The apostle Paul wrote, "And my God will supply all your needs according to His riches in glory in Christ Jesus" (Phil. 4:19). Our God is generous, and He takes pleasure in prospering us.

EL SHADDAI: THE GOD OF MORE THAN ENOUGH

Not only does God supply our needs, but He goes above and beyond. God does not want to see us barely scraping by in life. Our God is the Creator and source of all things in this world; there is never a shortage in His provision. God's resources are not just material things but also His abounding love, grace, strength, equipping, favor, healings, blessings, and miracles.

In Matthew 7:11, Jesus said, "If you then, being evil, know how to give good gifts to your children, how much more will your Father who is in heaven give good things to those who ask Him!" There are no limitations on God's supplies. He is the ultimate source and supplier of everything in every area of our lives. Our needs can never exceed His vast supplies or put a strain on His resources. He is God Almighty!

JEHOVAH RAPHA: THE GOD WHO HEALS US

God is our healer, in both body and soul. Psalm 147:3 says, "He heals the brokenhearted and binds up their wounds." The name Jehovah Rapha assures each of us that God wants to restore us to wholeness. David wrote, "Bless the LORD, O my soul, and forget none of His benefits; Who pardons all your iniquities, Who heals all your diseases" (Ps. 103:2–3, NASB). Nothing is too hard or too big for our God to heal and restore!

There are so many verses on healing, but I want to share a special few that I've repeated out loud while declaring my victory over cancer:

- You are the Lord that healeth me (Exod. 15:26).

- You will take sickness away from the midst of me, and the number of my days You will fulfill (Exod. 23:25–26).

- You sent Your Word and healed me and delivered me from my destructions (Ps. 107:20).

EL ROI: THE GOD WHO SEES ME

An Egyptian woman named Hagar was wandering alone in the wilderness, desperate to save the life of her son, Ishmael. The angel of the Lord appeared to her to bring her comfort. Hagar was so blessed that she cried out, "You are the God who sees me" (Gen. 16:13, NIV).

No matter how desperate our situation, we are never alone. Just as with Hagar, God sees us even in our darkest times and deepest troubles. What a comfort it is to know that God sees us and comes to bring us love, help, and a word of comfort.

JEHOVAH NISSI: THE LORD IS MY BANNER OF VICTORY

In military battles a banner or flag is held high to identify the allegiance of the soldiers. Jehovah Nissi, our Lord, declares that His name is on our banner identifying us as His own and declaring His victory for our battles! Psalm 60:4 says, "You have given a banner to those who fear You, that it may be displayed because of the truth. Selah."

The Lord's banner is displayed also as a sign of His great love.

King Solomon writes, "He brought me to the banqueting house, and his banner over me was love" (Song of Sol. 2:4).

Isaiah prophesied that Jesus would stand as a banner to the people in Isaiah 11:10. With this assurance we can confidently run and not grow weary and be filled with hope, peace, and joy.

JEHOVAH TSURI: GOD IS MY ROCK

God is described as our rock throughout the Psalms. He is immovable, unbreakable, a safe place for retreat, and a fortress in battle. God is our unlimited source of strength, firm foundation, support, and defense in all circumstances. "Trust in the LORD forever, for in GOD the LORD, we have an everlasting Rock" (Isa. 26:4, NASB).

You may remember that Hannah was barren, and she came to the temple in tears and cried in prayer, asking God to give her a child. When God gave her a son, Samuel, Hannah was overjoyed. Let's look at Hannah's prayer:

> And Hannah prayed and said: "My heart rejoices in the LORD; my horn is exalted in the LORD. I smile at my enemies, because I rejoice in Your salvation. No one is holy like the LORD, for there is none besides You, nor is there any rock like our God.
>
> —1 SAMUEL 2:1–2

Hannah smiled at her enemies, and in her hour of greatest need God was her rock like no one else.

JEHOVAH SABAOTH: THE LORD OF HOSTS

Jehovah Sabaoth translates as "The Lord of hosts," or "The Lord of armies," and appears more than 250 times in the Old Testament. Lord Sabaoth is sovereign over all physical and spiritual armies, including multitudes of angelic heavenly beings. Our God will rise up and conquer our adversaries, just as He did in Old Testament times.

As we face battles in our own lives, God Himself is fighting for us and with us. "If God be for us, who or what can be against us?" Nowhere is this demonstrated more than when David stood up to Goliath in the name of the Lord of hosts. Let's look at David's exact words when, as a teenager, he faced this giant:

> Then David said to the Philistine, "You come to me with a sword, with a spear, and with a javelin. But I come to you in the name of the LORD of hosts, the God of the armies of Israel, whom you have defied. This day the LORD will deliver you into my hand, and I will strike you and take your head from you. And this day I will give the carcasses of the camp of the Philistines to the birds of the air and the wild beasts of the earth, that all the earth may know that there is a God in Israel."
>
> —1 SAMUEL 17:45–46

David knew his only chance against Goliath was in the name of the Lord of hosts. We will conquer our giants too, including cancer, in the name of the Lord of hosts!

EL OLAM: THE ETERNAL GOD

Even before the creation of the universe, God existed. God has no beginning and no end. We are accustomed to telling time with clocks, calendars, and seasons, yet our God is not confined within time. The nature and character of God, His Word, His promises, His Kingdom, and all He stands for never changes. Nothing about God becomes outdated or loses relevance. His power and His priorities are eternal and never end.

Our God is faithful, dependable, and consistent. The Lord has eternity in sight for each of us someday, but He also has victory, impact, and purpose in this life on earth now.

King David wrote, "Lord, You have been our dwelling place in all generations...even from everlasting to everlasting, You are God" (Ps. 90:1–2). He is the same yesterday, today, and forever. (See Hebrews 13:8.)

JEHOVAH SHAMMAH: THE GOD WHO IS THERE

Wherever we go, whatever we face, whenever we need Him, Jehovah Shammah declares that "He is there"! Let this sink in deeply. Oftentimes we feel like we are out there facing circumstances all on our own. We may be desperately praying for God to show up and help us out, or begging Him to have mercy and come down from heaven to earth where we are and come to our aid.

David wrote that God was there no matter where he went.

> Where can I go from Your Spirit? Or where can I flee from Your presence? If I ascend into heaven, You are there; if I make my bed in hell, behold, You are there. If I take the wings of the morning, and dwell in the uttermost parts of the sea, even there Your hand shall lead me, and Your right hand shall hold me.
>
> —PSALM 139:7–10

Jehovah Shammah assures us that we are not alone. God Himself tells us His name Shammah actually means "I am there." He is telling us that His presence is not restricted to only certain places or to certain people. He is omnipresent, everywhere, and available to everyone who calls upon Him. In particular He is saying to you and me that His presence is with us at all times, in all places, and in all circumstances.

The beautiful thing about God's presence is that you experience His joy. David wrote, "In Your presence is fulness of joy; at Your right hand are pleasures forevermore" (Ps. 16:11).

We don't have to search far and wide or travel to faraway places seeking where God lives and "performs" His miracles. Where we go, He goes. Where we are, He is. What we are facing, He is facing with us. Wherever we are, He is there! His Spirit and presence are always with us, always available to us, and we are always welcome to enter into His holy place.

Whatever we need Him to be, wherever we need Him to be, Jehovah Shammah is the God who is there!

IMMANUEL: GOD IS WITH US

John 1:14 tells us how the prophecy of Isaiah 7:14 came to pass when Jesus, our Messiah, was born on the earth. "The Word became flesh and dwelt among us." He became Immanuel, "God with us."

When we celebrate Christmas and the birth of Jesus, we remember how Immanuel, "God with us," came to earth in the flesh. "'Behold, the virgin shall be with child, and bear a Son, and they shall call His name Immanuel,' which is translated, 'God with us'" (Matt. 1:23).

The apostle Paul wrote that God's presence is now inside of believers, which makes the Christian a living temple of God. How? God's Holy Spirit comes to live inside of us when we are born-again. First Corinthians 3:16 says, "Know ye not that ye are the temple of God, and that the Spirit of God dwelleth in you?" (KJV).

The Spirit of God lives within you and me. Stop and think about how truly amazing this is. What depth of love would cause God Almighty, Lord of all, King of all kings, to "become flesh and come and live among us" here on earth and within our hearts and bodies!

WHAT'S IN A NAME?

Everything we need or hope for is found in God's names. Almighty God is present and powerful! He desires to dwell within our hearts, have a relationship with us, and be actively involved with our lives.

If you meditate on the names of God, His Holy Spirit will reveal His nature and cover you and fill you with incredible comfort, confidence, and courage.

Let God Be God

Perhaps you can see more clearly now that our God is "God Almighty"! I trust the Lord to reveal Himself to you. For those of us who have had strong and faithful fathers, we can identify with the concept of God as our Father. If your human father has failed you or, worse, broken your heart, please know that God the Father in heaven desires earnestly to be your Father now. He will not break your heart but mend it. He will not fail you but do all He can to prove His love to you.

God's longing from the beginning of time, way back when He created Adam and Eve, was to have a family He could interact with, walk with, and grow with. God in heaven still desires to have a family, and He wants to adopt you! I encourage you to let God be God. Let Him adopt you and bring you into His family.

As I am writing this chapter, I am moved to tears feeling the love and awe of my Father's presence so strongly around me. I know that His Spirit is not here just for me to enjoy, but for you to sense as you read this. I feel Him drawing me and you closer to Him, even now.

Will You Pray With Me?

Father God, I come before You today and invite You into my heart. Thank You for wanting me as Your child. Thank You for adopting me. I turn away from all my sin and throw my addictions into the trash can where they belong. I choose to forgive people who've hurt me, just as You forgave people who hurt You and crucified You on the cross. Please forgive me for all I've ever done wrong. I give You my heart, soul, and life. I accept You as the Lord of my life and my future. Please make Yourself real to me. Fill my heart with Your hope, peace, joy, and courage. Holy Spirit, please come and live inside me. I receive Your supernatural healing into my soul, heart, and body. Make me a new

*person. Create in me a new and clean heart. Take me
to a new level in my walk and relationship with You. I
take the limits off You, and I take the limits off myself.
Let Your love and light overflow into me and through
me to shine to the world around me. As You bless me,
let me be a blessing to others. Thank You, Lord, for all
You are and all You are doing within me, for me, and
through me! Amen.*

I truly believe you are experiencing the Holy Spirit's sweet presence inside of you right now. His mercies are fresh every day. There is nothing stale, dry, or old school about our God—He is our Father, and He is God Jehovah. He promises, "I AM THAT I AM. I AM *all* that you need Me to be." (See Exodus 3:14.)

CHAPTER 13

IN AWE OF AN AWESOME GOD
TIZ HUCH

PEOPLE OFTEN SAY, "God is awesome," or, "Our God is an awesome God." There's even a song with that title. But what does it mean to be in awe of God?

AHA MOMENT

I'm sure you have heard of the modern term that someone is having an *aha moment*. *Merriam-Webster* describes *aha moment* as "a moment of sudden realization, inspiration, insight, recognition, or comprehension."[1]

In other words, we suddenly "get it," or a light bulb goes on in our minds, and in an instant a concept or new revelation is clear, bright, and makes sense. Perhaps a lightning bolt thought hits us and illuminates our mind with answers, direction, or understanding. Sometimes these moments are referred to as *epiphanies* or *wake-up calls*, a *moment of truth, internalizing,* or *owning a truth as your own.*

AWE-HA MOMENT

I don't know the origins of the term *aha moment*, but I believe it must be connected with the word *awe*. *Merriam-Webster* defines the word *awe* as "an emotion variously combining dread, veneration, and wonder that is inspired by authority or by the sacred or sublime."[2]

Leviticus 9:22–24 describes Aaron and the priests during a

time of worship when they fell on their faces out of fear, reverence, respect, awe, and wonder from the knowledge that God was in their midst.

Biblical references to the fear of God often also mean deep respect and reverential awe of realizing who He really is!

Merriam-Webster defines *awe* in its verb form to mean "inspired and filled with awe,"[3] as in being awed by the beauty of the mountains. I think a more accurate term of an aha moment would be an *awe*-ha moment!

KNOWING BRINGS PERSONAL OWNERSHIP AND POSSESSION OF HIS PROMISES

As pastors, Larry and I have seen these aha moments pass over our people's faces or show up in their words and body language as they hear the Word of God and experience an epiphany.

Oftentimes someone will say, "Pastor, I finally get it!"

There are Bible terms that refer to this same concept. The Greek word *logos* refers to the written Word of God. The Greek word *rhema* is also based upon the written Word of God but refers to the Word being spoken and brought to life and significance as it applies to a specific person or circumstance. We often refer to these as revelations that can cause a turning point, open new opportunities, or expand our limited perspective of our lives and futures.

This is the type of knowing that Jesus referred to in John 8:32 when He stated, "You shall *know* the truth and the truth will set you free" (emphasis added).

Larry and I can look back and point to every time we experienced one of these dynamic rhema, knowing, epiphany, wakeup, revelation, or aha moments that hit us in our hearts. As we owned the realities of His promises and truths, they have dynamically impacted us, set us free, and changed the course of our lives forever. We have experienced these points since we were both born-again decades ago. We've joyfully experienced these aha moments when God called us to ministry and we surrendered our futures to His will. Look at some of the revelations we've received in our aha moments:

- God is a good, loving, kind Father, not a mean, hard taskmaster.

- God is not a taker, He is a giver.

- God does not require us to take a vow of poverty but to take a vow of priorities.

You know, those eight thousand promises in the Bible belong to *you*. They belong to us too. We know today that God is Jehovah Rapha: the God who heals Lion *and* who heals me!

OUR AWE FOR GOD BECOMES OUR POINT OF REFERENCE TO HIM

To recap, the word *awe* has three different aspects of meaning:

- the power to inspire fear or dread (this is where the word *awful* originated)

- to be inspired or awestruck, such as by the beauty of creation

- respect, reverence, amazement, astonishment, or wonder inspired by authority or the sacred

The type of awe we have for the Lord becomes our point of reference to how we see God. The type of awe we have for God impacts how we see God, how we respond to Him, how we relate to Him, and how we expect to receive things from Him.

GOD THOUGHTS

Consider this. If we see God as vengeful, cruel, judgmental, a hard taskmaster, or uncaring, our perspective of Him will be filled with the awe of fear and dread. We don't want to be close to someone we fear or dread. Our response to knowing God will be one of apprehension.

If we see God as good and pleasant and appreciate Him, that is good but it's not really personal or a priority or relevant in our hearts. This kind of awe produces thoughts that God is there, but He is irrelevant in our lives, so we become indifferent to His presence and person.

If we see God as magnificent, all-powerful, sacred, and our loving Father, then our perspective of Him will be filled with the awe of sacred reverence, respect, amazement, astonishment, wonder, personal intimacy, hope, faith, confidence, inspiration, and expectation.

What are your everyday "God thoughts"?

What perspective of awe do you have for the Lord? Fearful, indifferent, casual, cautiously hopeful, intimate, faith-filled, expectant? An *awe-ha moment* with God and His promises can take us from awful and hopeless to awesome and hopeful. That awe-ha moment leaves us awestruck and assured of the fullness of His promises, blessings, and miracles to come in our own lives and futures!

BE STILL AND KNOW THAT HE IS GOD

These same awe-ha and aha moments are here for you too. No matter what you're facing, let the Spirit of God bring the promises of God to life within your heart right now. Take a moment to close your eyes, calm your mind, be still and "know" that He is God. (See Psalm 46:10.)

Pause and let it sink in deeply how much God loves you and how awesome He is. Own these truths personally. Let these biblical truths bring a moment of truth to your heart and life. But above all, try to grasp the reality and *awe* that God is real and that you are in His presence!

PRAY WITH ME

Pause for a moment right now and pray this prayer with me:

Father, I believe that You are real and that You love me and care about me. I take You at Your Word that You, Yourself, are watching over my life to perform Your Word and promises for me. I believe it, and I receive it into my heart, mind, body, and future right now. Thank You, Lord. Amen.

I hope you just experienced an awe-ha moment with the Lord. Did He enlarge your vision? Did He impress upon your heart to do something? Did He say something to you just now? Write it down. Take all the time you want or need to engage in conversation with God, because I sure am! Remember, the most important, life-altering moments of your day are those when you put aside everything and focus on God Almighty! In a world jam-packed with to-do lists, make sure you put "Spend time in His presence" at the top of your daily list. Stay awestruck in the presence of your awesome almighty God!

CHAPTER 14

PSALM 91 PROMISES IN A FALLEN WORLD
Tiz Huch

ON Tuesday morning, September 11, 2001, Americans watched with horror as one plane and then another crashed into the twin towers of the World Trade Center in New York City. By the time a third plane crashed in a suicide mission into the Pentagon in Washington, DC, that morning, all the world knew that America's mainland was under attack.

Oddly, the deadliest terrorist attack in US history occurred on 9/11, the very numbers all Americans know to dial on their phones to call for help in the event of a personal emergency. Indeed, frightened Americans inside the World Trade Center, Pentagon, and four passenger airplanes were dialing 911 on their cell phones to report this horrific emergency. Hundreds of people who were injured and trying to escape the flames and explosions called their loved ones. Newscasts repeatedly aired clips of the airplanes as they crashed into the twin towers. The nation was in a panic.

United Airlines Flight 93 crash-landed into a field in Shanksville, Pennsylvania, after passengers (while still in the air) overtook the terrorists who had hijacked the plane. All passengers and hijackers on board were killed, but the passengers' bravery likely saved the lives of hundreds more innocent Americans because the plane was said to be headed for Washington, DC. Within one hour, four passenger airliners exploded on American soil, and all innocent passengers as well as the terrorist hijackers were killed. Nearly three thousand people were killed and more than twenty-five thousand injured, including rescuers.

Church After 9/11

The Sunday following 9/11, churches all over America were packed, many to capacity. The nation was reeling from shock and grief. For the first time in decades, the majority of Americans went to church—and turned to God.

Larry and I pastored a church in Portland, Oregon, in 2001. Larry had to be out of town the end of September, so I taught the Sunday service. Anyone who remembers that September will tell you that our nation was turned upside down. Suddenly, our safe world in America was scary and unpredictable. Our minds were not just processing what happened on 9/11, but we all faced the uncertainty and even alarm at what else may be coming in the days ahead. *We had an enemy, but who were they? Why did they hate us? Would they attack again?*

I was heavily burdened about the far-reaching effects of 9/11. I knew God had given me a message based on Psalm 91 to bring hope, peace, and comfort to our people.

A Living Illustration of Protection

A few minutes before the service was to begin, a dear friend and church member came to the church office. For the sake of privacy, I'll call him Colonel Gerald. Gerald was a retired US Air Force colonel who had served during the Vietnam War. He and his best friend were both fighter pilots. Colonel Gerald told me that his friend served as a lead fighter pilot within the advanced level of elite air force squadrons. These squadrons had the highest casualty death rates in the air force due to the intense danger they faced head-on. These fighter pilots were the most highly trained and were sent on the most dangerous missions.

As a *lead* fighter pilot, his friend led his whole squadron of other fighter pilots into the direct line of fire of the enemy fighter pilots. Colonel Gerald's friend courageously led his squadron head-on, making them the frontline target of the enemy. I cannot even fathom how anyone could face down such fears and muster up the courage.

As our colonel friend continued this story, much to our relief, he reported that his friend was still alive all these years later and had made it through that terrible war with not even one injury. We all teared up as he told us that his friend was a deeply spiritual man, a man of serious prayer and faith. Every morning before suiting up for duty, he gathered his entire squad and had a time of prayer. He prayed for God's safety and protection over himself and his pilots. Guess what the main portion of their daily prayer was? They recited together the entire chapter of Psalm 91! This lead fighter pilot and his elite air force squadron had the lowest rate of death and injuries!

The dangers these pilots faced were about as intense and real as is earthly possible. However, the protection and defense that the Lord provided were as intense and real as is supernaturally possible.

That morning, as I taught on the reality and power of Psalm 91, I told this colonel's story. The testimony of this colonel and his friend gave me and our congregation the power to rise above and overcome the fear and dread that saturated America after 9/11.

If the verses of Psalm 91 could become real to those highly trained fighter pilots, then the same verses would certainly apply to our protection in the fall of 2001. Most of all, the promises of Psalm 91 are yours today—should you receive them for yourself.

PSALM 91

This beautiful psalm is an all-time favorite of many Christians. Let's read it together now:

> Whoever dwells in the shelter of the Most High will rest
> in the shadow of the Almighty. I will say of the LORD,
> "He is my refuge and my fortress, my God, in whom I

trust." Surely he will save you from the fowler's snare and from the deadly pestilence. He will cover you with his feathers, and under his wings you will find refuge; his faithfulness will be your shield and rampart. You will not fear the terror of night, nor the arrow that flies by day, nor the pestilence that stalks in the darkness, nor the plague that destroys at midday. A thousand may fall at your side, ten thousand at your right hand, but it will not come near you. You will only observe with your eyes and see the punishment of the wicked. If you say, "The LORD is my refuge," and you make the Most High your dwelling, no harm will overtake you, no disaster will come near your tent. For he will command his angels concerning you to guard you in all your ways; they will lift you up in their hands, so that you will not strike your foot against a stone. You will tread on the lion and the cobra; you will trample the great lion and the serpent. "Because he loves me," says the LORD, "I will rescue him; I will protect him, for he acknowledges my name. He will call on me, and I will answer him; I will be with him in trouble, I will deliver him and honor him. With long life I will satisfy him and show him my salvation."

—PSALM 91, NIV

Psalm 91 has stood the test of time as a sacred prayer and promise of God's presence, protection, and supernatural power in the lives of His people. It is amazing to me how the needs of the world are timeless and specific—and God's miracles are timeless and specific as well. It seems like Psalm 91 was written in reference to the world today as it talks of diseases and tumultuous times.

Remember, no challenge is too big or too small. God cares about us, and He will come to our rescue and release His miracles.

FEAR IS A PARALYZER

The strategy of the terrorists of 9/11 was not just to inflict a physical assault. The long-term goal was to release fear to paralyze the lives of Americans. Each year as the anniversary of 9/11 rolls around, we have only to look at television interviews of people injured or family members of people killed to see that we are still grieving the losses of 9/11. And we honor the victims of the attack. Besides the deaths and physical injuries, the mental and emotional stress created by terrorists is real.

After 9/11 the world basically drew to a halt out of fear of what else might be planned against us. The global economy, travel, business, stock markets, and employment were shaken. Fear became a paralyzing force.

In our own family, I remember that a simple trip to a public event or even the grocery store was first covered with prayer for the safety of our children. In our ministry, we ramped up our security teams for our church services and special events.

The morning of the 9/11 attacks, Larry was scheduled to fly to Atlanta for a conference he was to speak at. The flight was canceled, of course, but we later found out that that particular flight was likely to have been one of the flights targeted by the terrorists that day. Thank the Lord it was not! However, in the days and months to follow, our routine airline travel became a heightened concern. Even to this day, more than twenty years later, airport security is completely ramped up and revised compared to the days before 9/11.

FEAR IS A THIEF AND ROBBER

In 2022, our precautions and daily decisions are highly influenced by "terror attacks" in the health sector due to the global pandemic of the coronavirus—also called COVID-19. The loss of lives and the fear of contracting the disease or carrying it to others has caused waves of fear, destabilization, and paralysis across the world.

Fear paralyzes. Fear is a thief and robber in so many ways.

Fear of contracting the dreaded disease of COVID-19 robbed many people and families of celebrating simple things like birthdays, graduations, and Christmas. The government amplified fear of the disease by banning church services and social functions during a time when we most needed the support of one another. The fear of contracting or passing on the germs of COVID-19 was foremost in the minds of the world's citizens, evident by the millions of face masks sold to protect one another from exposure to the dreaded disease.

I am not saying we should not be respectful of one another's health, nor should we throw caution to the wind. Not by any means! My family and I took extreme precautions to avoid being exposed to COVID-19. Like most people, we wore masks, avoided physical contact with people in public, and postponed or canceled many of our plans and public events. We tried, like everyone else, to find a balance between biblical faith and plain old common sense.

In short, fear robs us of our normalcy and projects a series of "what ifs" into our future.

WILL PSALM 91 WORK TODAY?

The point I want to make is that the promises of our God that were spoken thousands of years ago during historically perilous times are true for you and me right now during our own perilous times. The strategies of terrorism haven't changed. Terrorism tries to paralyze us in fear, rob us of the blessings of God, and steal the destiny of God from our lives.

Whether we are facing war, financial instability, or health threats on a global level, we must be careful to resist fear. Worry and fear can saturate our thoughts until they overtake reasonable decision-making and rob us of God's peace. Our God is ready, willing, and able to save us! King David's God is our God, and He will protect, deliver, defend, and rescue us. He will bring us to victory in every area of our lives, whether physical, spiritual, or emotional. We must lay hold of the promises of God in every area:

- our health from a cold, COVID-19, cancer, or any other disease
- our family, marriage, and children
- our finances, jobs, and future
- our mind and emotions

Psalm 91 stands true for all of us and for all situations!

NAMES OF GOD IN PSALM 91

The names of God reveal the nature of God. Before we focus on what He can *do* for us, let's focus on who He is *to* us. Remember, we are not just seeking the miracles, we are seeking the Miracle worker.

Within this psalm are four names of God that signify four aspects of His protection. All four are used in the first two verses: God Almighty, the Most High, the Lord, and my God.

Most High

> Whoever dwells in the shelter of the Most High will rest in the shadow of the Almighty. I will say of the LORD, "He is my refuge and my fortress, my God, in whom I trust."
>
> —PSALM 91:1–2, NIV

The *Most High* is the ultimate authority who reigns supreme over everyone and everything. He is greater and higher than dangers, attacks, or negative reports. No matter what is terrorizing or intimidating you right now, our God is bigger, higher, and more powerful!

His name, the Most High, assures us that His power is higher and more potent than anything that comes against us. We are given the privilege to dwell in the shelter of the Most High.

Almighty

El Shaddai, *the Almighty*, declares His majesty and strength to confront and destroy every enemy. We may feel small and hopeless against the challenges we face, but our God is the Almighty, and He will come to our defense and destroy our enemies.

What is our position? Our position is one of rest. We are given the privilege of resting in the shadow of the Almighty as He fights our battles above us. He will lift us out of the battle to see it from His perspective if we ask Him.

Did you realize that before we even know we have a problem, God Almighty has already worked out the answer?

The Lord

The term *Lord* is a legal and political title. As Lord, our God takes precedence and dominion over all those forces that come against us.

You're not out there fighting your battles all alone. Our God goes before you and confirms His Word to you. No matter who or what is coming against you, God is in your corner. Psalm 97:10 assures us that "He guards the lives of His faithful." We are so privileged to have our Lord as our refuge and fortress!

My God

God Himself has chosen to associate intimately with those who trust Him and serve Him. Therefore, we can trust Him.

> "Because he loves me," says the LORD, "I will rescue him;
> I will protect him, for he acknowledges my name. He
> will call on me, and I will answer him; I will be with
> him in trouble, I will deliver him and honor him. With
> long life I will satisfy him and show him my salvation."
> —PSALM 91:14–15, NIV

Doesn't that just calm your heart and move your soul to tears? Yes, He is the God of the entire world, for all times and all generations. That is how great He is. But He is also *our* God! He loves each of us, and we can trust Him with our life and future,

PSALM 91 RELEVANCE TODAY

We live in times of pandemics, threats of global wars, financial upheavals, and job uncertainties. Ungodliness surrounds us in our schools, workplaces, media, and culture. Values, morals, decency, honesty, and integrity are rare in the twenty-first century. The solid foundations that once belonged to the church and society are slipping away beneath us. How should we respond?

WE LIVE IN A FALLEN WORLD

There is no place in the Bible where we are told that our earthly life will be completely trouble-free. We are in this world, but we are not of this world. However, we live in the realities of a fallen world and are, to some degree, affected by the perils and pitfalls of our world. The enemy of God and of our souls comes to steal, kill, and destroy that which is precious to God. The society we live in blatantly tries to eliminate God and the principles of His Word from the face of the earth. It is the age-old story of the Bible from the beginning of time.

Psalm 91 has become especially relevant these past few years because of the COVID-19 pandemic. We have all been faced with this "deadly pestilence that stalks in darkness." It has been an unpredictable, unwelcome, and forceful adversary. Verses 5, 6, and 7 have risen to a new level of relevance in the prayer lives of many, including me and my family. These words are not just old stories on the pages of an ancient book. These verses are meant to be taken literally and carry life and power that can protect our lives. Are you fighting a sickness? Declare these verses in Psalm 91:

> You will not fear the terror of night, nor the arrow that
> flies by day, nor the pestilence that stalks in the dark-
> ness, nor the plague that destroys at midday. A thousand
> may fall at your side, ten thousand at your right hand,
> but it will not come near you.
>
> —PSALM 91:5–7, NIV

Cancer delivered some tough battles to our family, that's for sure. At the same time, just like the rest of the world, we also went through the same upheavals from the pandemic. But God brought us through it all, didn't He? Many years ago God's Word came out of the pages of our Bible and lodged in our hearts. In our day of battle, those promises came up out of our hearts and into our mouths, and together Larry and I declared the living Word of God! And praise God, He released His miracles by the moment!

SATURATE YOUR MIND WITH GOD'S PROMISES NOT PROBLEMS

Let me say this again. Faith doesn't mean we close our eyes in denial and pretend problems don't exist. Faith means we open our eyes in faith and pray God's promises into existence.

Standing in faith doesn't mean we throw out common sense either.

While we diligently pray and trust God to protect us from the "pestilence and plagues," we are also diligent to wash our hands, wear a mask, and use common sense.

My motto through the COVID-19 pandemic has been "Pray hard and wash your hands!"

In fighting cancer, my immune system was very compro-mised, making me susceptible to infections, viruses, and germs. Larry and I did not feel one bit of conflict between living by faith versus being smart. As we've said before, believing in God and believing in science are not meant to be in opposition to each other. We fought cancer by faith, and then we did everything possible in the medical and natural arenas to fight the cancer that had attacked Lion's body and then mine. We can testify that we saw God put His *super* to our *natural*!

Do not let your heart be saturated with the bad news of the world. Instead, make a point to become saturated by the good news of God's Word. Rather than allowing the bad reports to become an anchor that weighs you down, let the good news of God's Word anchor your soul and steady you during the storms all around you.

As I mentioned before, "All the water in the oceans cannot sink a ship unless it gets inside." This is one of my favorite sayings. No matter how much stormy water surrounds our lives, it cannot sink us unless it gets inside of us. This is a great example of why we need to be so careful of what stormy news we allow entry into our hearts and thoughts. We do have to process through challenging issues, of course, but filter it all through the promises of God and His Word.

If you read Psalm 91 and pray it out loud daily for a week or even a month, your faith will rise. You will discover that when bad news comes to your ears, Psalm 91 will arise in your heart. My friend, saturate your mind with God's Word and let it arise and fight your battles for you!

CHAPTER 15

DON'T LIMIT WHAT GOD CAN DO

Larry Huch

I LOVE WHAT Tiz says: "For every mountain there's a miracle. For every problem there's a promise." My wife can teach and preach! But that is because she lives it and walks it out in everyday life. You've read Tiz's in-depth teaching on faith and watched our family's miracles by the moment unfold. Just in case you are still not totally in the fight of faith, I want to come alongside you now for the remaining chapters of this book and help you fight like a *real* Christian soldier!

THE FIST OF FAITH

I don't like the mindset that Christians are supposed to be sweet, mellow, wishy-washy people. We ought to be kind and full of love, but that doesn't mean we let the world and the devil walk all over us. Before I gave my life to the Lord, I was a street fighter. When I became a Christian, I didn't become a sissy. I'm still a street fighter; it's just that I'm fighting the devil instead of people. The Word of God tells us to take the kingdom of heaven by force.

> And from the days of John the Baptist until now the kingdom of heaven suffers violence, and the violent take it by force.
>
> —Matthew 11:12

You see, the devil is going to come against you, but the violent will take the victory over him by force. There are times when you are fighting the adversary that you must raise your fist of faith and knock down that giant that is blaspheming God. Faith is a muscle. If you use it, you get stronger in your faith, and if you don't use it, you get weaker in your faith.

When my family was attacked with these recent health challenges, a righteous indignation rose up within me in a violent, take-it-by-force way! Everything within me rose up to fight, conquer, and overcome these battles! I felt as if I were in a boxing match and had gotten sucker punched. I felt as though the wind got punched right out of me. But I immediately caught my breath and went to war.

In the physical realm there was not a person or thing to fight. In the spiritual realm there was plenty to fight! I'm going to teach you in these next chapters how to gird up and fight your own challenges; overcome the attacks against your life, family, finances, and future; and win every battle that ever comes against you!

God's men and women are not to be angry, violent, and out of control in destructive ways. However, we are meant to be angry against sin and injustice; be violent against the enemies of God and His people; and focus our intensity on faith-filled constructive ways that change the course of our lives and of the world for the good and the glory of God!

But faith can also be a negative force. Sometimes because people don't know how to fight a difficult battle, they become stronger in negative faith. Sometimes being negative is just a habit or pattern. We need to recognize it and its destructive force in order to counteract it and release the constructive force of positive faith. You and I want to be strong in positive faith. Do not limit God!

IS ANYTHING TOO HARD FOR THE LORD?

Romans 4:16 calls Abraham the father of faith, and the father of us all. Let's look at just one day in the life of Abraham and his wife, Sarah. On this particular day the Lord Himself and two other men or angels showed up at their home. Abraham was sitting at the door of his tent and saw them coming. Let's pick up this story in Genesis 18:

> Then they said to him, "Where is Sarah your wife?" So he said, "Here, in the tent." And He said, "I will certainly return to you according to the time of life, and behold, Sarah your wife shall have a son." (Sarah was listening in the tent door which was behind him.) Now Abraham and Sarah were old, well advanced in age; and Sarah had passed the age of childbearing. Therefore Sarah laughed within herself, saying, "After I have grown old, shall I have pleasure, my lord being old also?" And the Lord said to Abraham, "Why did Sarah laugh, saying, 'Shall I surely bear a child, since I am old?' Is anything too hard for the Lord? At the appointed time I will return to you, according to the time of life, and Sarah shall have a son." But Sarah denied it, saying, "I did not laugh," for she was afraid. And He said, "No, but you did laugh!"
>
> —GENESIS 18:9–15

Now, most people who tell this story always tell the part where Sarah laughed, but if you go to the previous chapter, you'll see that Abraham laughed at this promise as well. Genesis 17:17 says, "Then Abraham fell on his face and laughed, and said in his heart, 'Shall a child be born to a man who is one hundred years old? And shall Sarah, who is ninety years old, bear a child?'"

This makes me wonder why it is that today when we share this story, we always talk about how Sarah laughed and didn't have faith. But here is Abraham, who is later referred to as the father of faith, and he laughed too!

AT THE APPOINTED TIME

Let's look at Genesis 18:14 one more time. The Lord said to Abraham, "Is anything too hard for the LORD? At the *appointed time* I will return to you, according to the time of life, and Sarah shall have a son" (emphasis added).

How many of us have prayed and prayed and prayed about something, and it doesn't seem like it's going to happen. It's almost there, but we give up right before God's appointed time. If you are in a difficult battle right now and you have prayed and believed God, but you haven't yet seen victory, I want you to remember that God's ways are not our ways, and God's timing is not our timing. Sometimes it takes what God sees as "the fullness of time" or "the appointed time." You see, patience that is developed in waiting for your answer from God will bring you to a perfect work of God in your life:

> ...knowing that the testing of your faith produces patience. But let patience have its perfect work, that you may be perfect and complete, lacking nothing. If any of you lacks wisdom, let him ask of God, who gives to all liberally and without reproach, and it will be given to him.
> —JAMES 1:3–5

I love it when I pray and God answers immediately. Sometimes He does, and I love that! I love it when we pray, God's already sending the answer, and before the prayer is finished the answer is already there. But there are times when God wants to do more than just answer our prayer. This is what it means in James when it says, "Let patience have its perfect work."

WHEN GOD WANTS TO GIVE YOU MORE

Abraham and Sarah had been praying for a long time for a son, but God didn't want to just give them a son, He wanted to give them a son named Isaac. The same is true of Hannah. Hannah was praying for a son. Her husband had two wives, and this other lady had all these children. She even mocked Hannah, but Hannah was serving the Lord and was so faithful.

Finally, Hannah said, "Lord, why won't You give me a son? If You give me a son, I'll give him back to You, and he'll serve You."

You see, sometimes God wants to give you more than you've requested. God didn't want to just give Hannah a son, God wanted to give Hannah *Samuel*. He wanted to give her a prophet. When God is getting ready to do something bigger than what we can even ask or think, sometimes He waits a while so that we get out of the way or so that the promise comes at the appointed time. God sees what we cannot see, and when your miracle happens, you will know it was God.

Do you understand what I'm saying? We're living in a time the world has been waiting for. We're surrounded by so great a cloud of witnesses. You and I are surrounded, and above us in the balcony of heaven Abraham and Sarah, Hannah, Esther, Jacob, Moses, Daniel, Ezekiel, Peter, Paul, and John are all looking down on us right now. I believe they are saying, "It was great the way God used us, but I would that I could be where these people are right now."

I don't know about you, but the last seven years were the toughest in our lives—the toughest in our family, our ministry, and our finances. Why? Because God is getting ready to do something more than we're asking for. Like Hannah, we are asking for a son, but He's about to birth us a prophet. This applies to you too. God wants to birth you a miracle that is beyond anything, and this miracle will never go away—never.

SOMETIMES GOD'S DELAY IS NOT GOD'S DENIAL

Sometimes God's delay is not God's denial. But what mistake do we make that we see Abraham and Sarah make? God comes and says, "This is what I'm going to do for you." What did they do? They rehearsed all the reasons why it couldn't happen.

Don't limit what God can do by reminding God of all the

reasons that it can't happen. "I'm going to give you a son, and I'm going to return." Sarah laughed. Abraham laughed.

God says to Sarah, "Why did you laugh?"

Sarah says, "I didn't laugh."

Sarah laughed at what God said. Talk about bad timing. She said, "How can this happen? How can I have pleasure?"

Now, I don't know if she was laughing because she was looking at Abraham, but something was going on. She began to rehearse all the reasons why it couldn't happen:

- I'm beyond childbearing.

- I'm old.

- Abraham's old.

- He's not even interested.

We do the same thing. You know what? God can do something for you. God can break this through. We are tempted to rehearse all the reasons why it can't happen:

- Well, how can it happen?

- Have you seen what the economy says?

- Have you seen what the newspapers said?

- Have you seen what this report says?

- Have you seen what that cancer diagnosis says?

Let all men be liars, but let what God says be true! Don't limit what God can do. It's called faith. I've seen people who feel threatened by faith. Sometimes even religious people are threatened by faith.

A person feeling threatened by faith may look at you and say (or think), "You're just being arrogant, presumptuous, or cocky." For over forty-five years, Tiz and I have lived our lives pushing the limits of faith in our God, His promises, and His power. True faith takes boldness, courage, and deliberate choices. When we choose to take the limits off our God, the limits come off our lives, circumstances, and futures! Each step forward in faith takes us to new levels of confidence, dominion, and authority in the spiritual realm. Each victory develops and strengthens our faith and trust in God.

YOUNG DAVID—THE LEAST OF HIS FAMILY

King David wasn't always looked upon as the king. He was the runt of the litter. He was the least likely to succeed in Jesse's house. How do we know this? We know that David's family didn't consider him as worthy because when Samuel came to visit Jesse's home, he asked Jesse to bring his sons before him.

> Thus Jesse made seven of his sons pass before Samuel. And Samuel said to Jesse, "The LORD has not chosen these." And Samuel said to Jesse, "Are all the young men here?" Then he said, "There remains yet the youngest, and there he is, keeping the sheep." And Samuel said to Jesse, "Send and bring him. For we will not sit down till he comes here."
>
> —1 SAMUEL 16:10–11

Dad brought in all the older brothers. They were strong, tall, athletic, smart, and handsome. And the prophet said, "No, it's not him. No, it's not him."

When Samuel asks if Jesse brought all of his sons before him, Jesse replies, "Well, I've got David."

God loves to use the ones who are least likely. Do you understand? Listen to what I'm saying, because God would love to open the windows of blessings over you, because people will say, "How in the world could that happen for you?"

You can reply, "Well, let me tell you about my God. And what He has done for me, He can do for you too!"

But see, this was David. David wasn't even brought in on the showing. David was ordered to go out there, away from the presence of the famous prophet Samuel, and take care of the family's sheep. David was the youngest and least significant of all the brothers. In the eyes of his family, he was the least qualified among them. In the eyes of the Lord, he was the most qualified among them!

We know the story of David and Goliath. I've been at this actual geographic location in Israel many times. There is a flat plateau on one side and a flat plateau on the other side, with a little valley in between. It's maybe one hundred to two hundred yards across. The Philistine army camped on one side, and Israel's army camped on the other side—and David killed Goliath right there on the ground in the middle. I've picked up stones from that location.

A lot of people don't realize the size of Goliath. He was nine and a half feet tall. The head on his spear weighed eighteen and a half pounds. A shot put weighs twelve pounds, so imagine the head of a spear at eighteen and a half pounds! Just his coat of chain mail, which had overlapping metal links down his chest, weighed 160 pounds. This guy was massive, and he was standing out there yelling at the Israelites, God's people. David was a young boy, only about fourteen years old. He probably was as tall as Goliath's waist and belly button.

WHO DO YOU THINK YOU ARE?

Understand, our Goliath is the devil, the enemy of our life. Goliath is the one who was saying, "I'll kill you. I'm going to kill your job. I'm going to kill your business. I'm going to kill your economy. I'm going to ruin your family and annihilate your future and the future of those you love!"

Goliath was out there threatening while God's army, the trained soldiers, were in their tents. David was bringing his brothers' lunch. He's like the pizza delivery boy. He was bringing the cheese and bread. David shows up and sees the threats Goliath is making.

Today we see the attacks of poverty, debt, lack, fear, racism, discrimination, anger, hatred, violence, drug addiction, bondages, sin, immorality, rebellion, corruption, divorce, and division in families. We see the enemy of sickness, disease, leukemia, ovarian cancer, and other illnesses threatening the futures of God's people. Like David, we see it all out there challenging us—and challenging God's people. How will we respond? How did David respond?

David steps up and says, "Who is this uncircumcised Philistine?" He didn't say, "Who is this guy who's nine and a half feet tall, whose spearhead is eighteen and a half pounds, whose chain mail weighs 160 pounds."

No, David didn't analyze or rehearse all the large, visible obstacles and challenges.

David said, "Who is this guy who has no covenant with God?" That's what he was saying. "Who is this uncircumcised Philistine to defy the armies of the living God?"

Do you know what his brothers and the other soldiers of Israel said? They said, "You cocky little guy. Who do you think you are?"

David knew that it wasn't who he was, but who his God was. David had a covenant with God, and Goliath didn't. From David's point of view, Goliath was already defeated and had already lost.

Let me ask you today. Who do you think you are? Are you in covenant with God? Is your enemy making loud noises right now and taunting you? How do you see yourself in relation to the challenges you're facing? Do you see yourself as helpless or empowered by God Almighty? Do you envision defeat or victory? Do you see your enemy as undefeatable or as already defeated by God your Father? Do you see the enormous size of your Goliath or the enormous size of your God? Of course, when we look through the eyes of the natural realm, we are intimidated, fearful, and filled with anxiety. But when we look through the eyes of the supernatural realm, we are encouraged, empowered, and filled with faith!

Notice that when David was questioned, he gave his testimonies right away. He told the king and the other soldiers what God did for him when he was all alone caring for his dad's sheep.

TELL YOUR TESTIMONY

When David was told he couldn't fight Goliath, he recounted the stories of how God protected him previously in his life.

David said, "When I was out there alone tending to the sheep, a lion came and stole one of my father's sheep. I went up there and took it back and killed that lion. Then a bear came and stole a sheep. I tracked him down and killed him too."

My friend, what has that lion stolen from you? What has that bear stolen from you? Give me back that sheep! It's mine! The Bible says he took the sheep right out of the predator's mouth.

"Who do you think you are?" they asked David.

David said, "I'll tell you who I am. I'm the one that saw God help me face down and defeat a lion and then a bear." You see, great giant-killing faith is built by smaller acts of faith that build up your experiences of confidence and courage, which lead to larger experiences of victories!

One of the best things you can do when you're about to face your fight with Goliath (the enemy or life's circumstances) is to tell the people around you what God did for you in previous days of your life. It builds their faith and your own faith and confidence.

I love this story, and I love David. David picks up a stone, a rock. That rock is a representative of God's Word. Jesus defeated the devil in the wilderness. When the devil came after Jesus and tempted Him, Jesus defeated him by saying, "But the Word of God says..." That rock represents Jesus Christ, His Word, and His covenant promise with you.

David was not an expert rock flinger. But because David partnered with God, God's power was behind that stone, and when it flew into the air, it landed in the one open spot in Goliath's armor, and *boom*—David and God took that giant out.

But the thing I love about David is that he didn't pick up one rock. He picked up five smooth stones. Why? Goliath had four brothers.

When David picked up five stones, his heart was saying, "My God is going to do exceedingly, abundantly above all I can imagine. When I'm done with Goliath, I'm coming for you and you and you and *you* too!"

Are you facing a giant of debt or sickness or strife? Pick up more than one stone, because when God's done with defeating debt, He's coming to defeat sickness. When He's done defeating divorce, then He's coming to defeat anger. Pick up your stones and declare who God is and what He is going to do for you. Keep throwing those rocks, and that Goliath and his brothers are coming down!

MY FIST OF FAITH TESTIMONY

Remember, from the days of John the Baptist until now the kingdom of heaven suffers violence, and the violent take it by force (Matt. 11:12). *You* are the kingdom of heaven, and the devil is going to fight you, but you must get up and fight back.

Like David said, our fight is fixed. The enemy is already defeated. Goliath will come down—if you fight. *If* is the operative word here. If you fight, it's fixed.

Many years ago, and many, many pounds ago, I fought in the Golden Gloves boxing tournament in Chicago. Growing up in South St. Louis, boxing was a big part of my aggressive inner-city lifestyle.

In those days, you weighed in about two hours before you fought. Then they wrapped your hands so you wouldn't do anything or add anything into your gloves. Then you had to go sit in what's called the box, close to the ring, and you had to sit next to the guy you were going to fight.

I'm a little white guy, seventeen years old, sitting next to this guy who's got a five o'clock shadow, and it's nine in the morning. This guy's got scars on his face. He looks over at me, and to my amazement, he's got no teeth! This guy has to be thirty years old. I find out that he's been picked by *Ring* magazine to win a medal in the Olympics—and this is my first fight.

This guy's glaring at me as if to say, *"Are you kidding me?"*

My manager comes over and whispers in my ear, "He's made to order for you."

I'm thinking, "Yeah, if I want to die, this is perfectly made to order for me!"

Then I decided, "You know what? I can't get up there and dance with this guy. This guy is so much bigger and older than me. The only thing I can do is just hit him and keep on hitting him."

We get in the ring, and he's big. The bell rings, and I run out there and start punching him with everything I've got. I knocked him out in fifty-four seconds into the first round of my very first fight. It's true. I knocked him out. But I learned something—if you're in a fight, *fight*! Just like "from the days of John the Baptist till now," the devil's going to fight you, so you'd better learn how to fight and take your victory by force!

FAITH IS A MUSCLE

When my grandkids were little, they would stay with us every weekend. We had boxing gloves for all of our grand-sugars, and they loved to box! Even little Aviva Shalom loved to box.

One time when Aviva was about four years old, she ran up and punched me without a boxing glove. She cheap-shotted me and hit me from behind in the kidneys.

She said, "Ooooouch!"

I said, "What?"

She said, "I hurt my hand."

I said, "Let me see how you make a fist." She made a fist and put her thumb inside of her fist.

"No, no, sweetie," I said, "when you make a fist, you've got to keep that thumb out."

I want to show you how to make a fist too so that when you hit the devil, he's going down. Now, you may feel like you're in the twelfth round, but I'm telling you, the fight is almost over. You can believe that. The fight is almost over, so let's knock the devil out.

Faith is a muscle. As I said earlier in this chapter, if you use your faith, it will get stronger and stronger. If you don't use your faith, you will get weaker in faith.

Don't limit what God can do. Peter and the boys were out fishing all night long, and they caught nothing. Now, this is an example of what many of us have gone through—myself included. Perhaps you are thinking, the last several years I've been working hard but have caught nothing. My friend, let me assure you, your Jesus will show up.

I believe God allowed some of us to go through some of the things we've gone through so that we get to the end of ourselves, and we have to say, "God, it's You." Because the danger is that we can forget it's Him.

Jesus comes on the shore, and Peter's been out with John all night fishing. Jesus stands on the shore. "How's the fishing, boys?" That's like the day the Lord said to Abraham, "Where is Sarah?"

You see, the Lord knows everything. He wasn't asking where Sarah was physically; He was asking where Sarah was spiritually, concerning this miracle.

I want to talk to you for a moment about developing your faith muscle in your marriage.

FAITH IS A MUSCLE IN MARRIAGE

God dealt with Abraham first and said to him, "You're going to have a child." Abraham fell over laughing. But obviously Abraham wasn't there yet in his faith because he hadn't even shared God's promise with Sarah yet. Where was Sarah on this?

Listen to me, if you're married, get together on this. I'm going to tell you something that is a secret to our marriage and our ministry. Serving God is so easy for us because even as my wife and I went through Lion's diagnosis of leukemia and then her diagnosis of ovarian cancer, Tiz and I were always on the same page. We are not in conflict—we're together in our faith. We are yoked together. God's promise is the yoke, and we're going all the way with what God says.

My friend, get together with your spouse, and don't allow

times of battle to cause you to fight with each other or quarrel with each other. Get together and believe God together. Jesus told us in Matthew 18:19, "If two of you agree on earth concerning anything that they ask, it will be done for them by My Father in heaven." Another passage states, "Where two or three are gathered together in my name, I am there in the midst of them" (Matt. 18:20). I don't know about you, but I want to be where God is, and I want God to be in the center of our marriage.

Develop your faith muscle in your marriage and get into agreement. Your home needs to be the sanctuary of faith. That's prophetic! Your home needs it. Are you facing an attack or a negative message on your door? If so, when you cross over the threshold of your home, leave that message and all its problems outside. When you walk into your home, talk about what God can do, what God's going to do, and the miracle you will get. Don't get inside the house and start talking about how old you are and how barren you are and how ugly Abraham is. Get together. Get in agreement! That's what the Lord was doing with Sarah and Abraham.

He said, "Where is Sarah on this? Abraham, where are you on this, and where is Sarah on this?" They had to come together.

Tiz and I know what it is to face some hard times. You may be facing one of the hardest times in your life right now, but I'm telling you something. The Lord is about to show up. God wanted you to pick up this book and read this chapter today. Don't you limit what God can do.

If God said, "I'm going to fill the net," He's going to fill the net. If God said, "Water's coming out of a rock," water is coming out of that rock. If God said, "The baskets will be multiplied," the baskets will be multiplied. If God said, "A prophet is coming out of your womb," then He will do it. (See Luke 5:4–6; John 21:6–8; Numbers 20:11; John 6:11–13; 1 Samuel 1.)

If God said, "I am the Lord that healeth thee," then He is going to fulfill that promise!

Do not let the devil or the world walk all over you. You are in a covenant promise with God Most High. Take the kingdom of heaven by force!

CHAPTER 16

DON'T LIMIT HOW GOD CAN DO IT

LARRY HUCH

JESUS MADE IT clear to us that the kingdom of heaven experiences violence. There is a war going on in the heavenlies. When our baby grandson, Lion, woke up in the night screaming with pain and fever, there was a war in the heavenlies. When Tiz felt pain in her abdomen while we were in Israel, there was a war going on in the heavenlies.

Jesus said in Matthew 11:12, "And from the days of John the Baptist until now the kingdom of heaven suffers violence, and the violent take it by force." Now, what does that mean? That means there's a real devil and he knows that he can't stop you from going to heaven because you are God's child. So his tactic is to steal, kill, and destroy everything that's already ours through the blood of Jesus Christ.

Sometimes people think that if you have faith, you don't go through battles. Faith does not mean there are no battles. *Faith* means that no matter what battle you face, you win. You and I have faith in some measure. The problem is, too many of us have negative faith.

Two blind men approached Jesus one day and cried out for mercy. They followed Jesus, and the Bible says that Jesus kept walking until He went inside a house. Let's read what happened next.

> And when He had come into the house, the blind men
> came to Him. And Jesus said to them, "Do you believe
> that I am able to do this?" They said to Him, "Yes, Lord."
> Then He touched their eyes, saying, "According to your
> faith let it be to you." And their eyes were opened.
>
> —MATTHEW 9:28–30

Notice that the Lord said, "According to your faith let it be to
you." I wish it meant that if you have positive faith then all good
things will happen, but if you have negative faith nothing will
happen. But that's not what it means. God is no respecter of persons. If He'll bless one, He'll bless another. But when God gives a
promise, there is our part of having faith in that promise. As Tiz
always says "There is God's part, and there is our part."

NEGATIVE FAITH OR POSITIVE FAITH?

If you recall, God told Moses to send out twelve spies to look
over the land God promised to His people. Moses was very specific about what he wanted to know in their report.

> Then Moses sent them to spy out the land of Canaan,
> and said to them, "Go up this way into the South,
> and go up to the mountains, and see what the land is
> like: whether the people who dwell in it are strong or
> weak, few or many; whether the land they dwell in is
> good or bad; whether the cities they inhabit are like
> camps or strongholds; whether the land is rich or poor;
> and whether there are forests there or not. Be of good
> courage. And bring some of the fruit of the land." Now
> the time was the season of the first ripe grapes.
>
> —NUMBERS 13:17–20

The twelve spies returned, and they all agreed that the land
flowed with milk and honey. However, ten of the spies sent a
ripple of fear throughout the Israelite camp with their negative
faith. Let's look at the report from those ten spies:

The land through which we have gone as spies is a land
that devours its inhabitants, and all the people whom
we saw in it are men of great stature. There we saw the
giants (the descendants of Anak came from the giants);
and we were like grasshoppers in our own sight, and so
we were in their sight.

—NUMBERS 13:32–33

Their report is a picture of negative faith. Caleb quieted the
people down and said, "Let us go up at once and take possession,
for we are well able to overcome it."

Caleb and Joshua were the only two who saw God as larger
than the giants in the land. Caleb and Joshua had faith to take
the land and conquer the giants.

The ten spies went out and said, "We can see the land *but*"—
and there's the problem right there. That word *but* is a signal that
negative faith is coming God's way. "We see the land. It's just like
God said, *but... But* the economy, *but* this, *but* that."

God never said there weren't going to be any giants. He just
said, "I am a giant killer."

A MEASURE OF FAITH

Romans 12:3 says that God has dealt to each one of us a measure of faith, and we are not to be proud of our measure, but
humble. God will not bless a proud person, and it's important to
stay humble before Him and not think of ourselves more highly
than we ought to think.

To every one of us He's given a measure of faith. You may
visualize this as someone handing out cards around the table
during a family card game. When we are conceived, God says
here's faith, here's faith, here's faith, here's faith, here's faith,
here's faith, here's faith, here's faith. He gives everybody in His
family a measure of faith. But if we don't use the measure of faith
God gave us, it atrophies. As a matter of fact, it's worse than that.
Our faith can actually go in the opposite direction. Instead of

having faith in God and all His promises, we start having faith in the economy and faith in what we see, feel, and smell. Then we become strong in negative faith.

JUBILEE IS COMING

We are about to enter into the most exciting time in the history of the world. I believe 1,000 percent that we're heading into the messianic era. I'm not saying when the Messiah is coming, but I'm saying in this era He's coming.

This is it. This is what we've been waiting for. This is why we're surrounded by so great a cloud of witnesses. They know that what we are about to witness is tremendous!

I'm emphasizing faith because God wants to make sure we don't miss the most exciting time to be alive! God is about to have a party, and you and I are invited. The devil's going to try to stop it, so we need to learn how to make a fist of faith to knock the devil out.

You've got to understand that from the days of John the Baptist until now, the devil is going to fight against the children of God, but the violent will take the devil down by force. We need to be more aggressive in our Christianity.

DON'T LIMIT WHAT GOD CAN DO

We do not want to limit what God can do. As a pastor I see this all the time—people rehearse all the reasons why God can't do what He said He would do. A lot of saints sound like Sarah when she said, "Well, how can I have a child when I'm old and my husband's not even interested? And I'm not interested in him?" That's what people do.

I love living a life where the natural cannot limit us. We live with a supernatural God. He is above and beyond the natural. When God says He's going to do something, don't rehearse excuses to God and tell Him why it can't happen. Don't tell God, "Well, I'm old, and my husband and I are beyond the age." No!

If God says you're going to have a child, you're going to have a child.

God's response to Sarah was, "Is anything too hard for the LORD?" (Gen. 18:14).

My family and I live by faith, and it's a fun way to live. Faith has to be developed, but I'm going to be honest with you. No matter what we're looking at or what God's calling us to do, with God all things are possible. That's the thumb. You've got to put the thumb on the outside of your fist or you'll break your thumb.

Tiz always says, "Don't wait until you need a miracle to learn how to get a miracle."

I say, "Don't wait until you're in a fight to learn how to fight."

I thank God that when we faced these battles with health, we had a long history of knowing the power of spiritual warfare and pressing in to the promises of God. It's never too late to start learning and practicing them.

There are biblical, age-old, tried-and-true spiritual weapons of our warfare that work for us—and will work for you.

The first finger in your fist of faith is this: don't limit what God can do.

THE SPIRITUALLY ARROGANT WILL RESIST GOD'S METHODS

The second finger in your fist of faith is do not limit how God can do it. To understand this concept, I want to look at one of the greatest stories in all of God's Word—the story of Naaman the leper. As we read this story, keep in mind that Naaman had spiritual arrogance. He wanted to be healed, but he wanted God to perform the healing his way.

It's important to know that the Hebrew word for *leper* used here is *tzaraat,* which was a leprous bodily manifestation that resulted from a spiritual condition such as arrogance, among other sins.[1] In biblical times, lepers were put outside the camp. They could still see the camp, and they could see the blessing in the camp, but they couldn't be a part of the camp. Spiritually speaking, I'm saying let's get rid of the leprosy of spiritual arrogance and get back in the camp of God's blessing.

Let's read Naaman's story from 2 Kings.

> Now Naaman, commander of the army of the king of Syria, was a great and honorable man in the eyes of his master, because by him the LORD had given victory to Syria. He was also a mighty man of valor, but a leper. And the Syrians had gone out on raids, and had brought back captive a young girl from the land of Israel. She waited on Naaman's wife. Then she said to her mistress, "If only my master were with the prophet who is in Samaria! For he would heal him of his leprosy." And Naaman went in and told his master, saying, "Thus and thus said the girl who is from the land of Israel."
>
> Then the king of Syria said, "Go now, and I will send a letter to the king of Israel." So he departed and took with him ten talents of silver, six thousand shekels of gold, and ten changes of clothing. Then he brought the letter to the king of Israel, which said, Now be advised, when this letter comes to you, that I have sent Naaman my servant to you, that you may heal him of his leprosy.
>
> And it happened, when the king of Israel read the letter, that he tore his clothes and said, "Am I God, to kill and make alive, that this man sends a man to me to heal him of his leprosy? Therefore please consider, and see how he seeks a quarrel with me."
>
> So it was, when Elisha the man of God heard that the king of Israel had torn his clothes, that he sent to the king, saying, "Why have you torn your clothes? Please let him come to me, and he shall know that there is a prophet in Israel."
>
> Then Naaman went with his horses and chariot, and he stood at the door of Elisha's house.
>
> —2 KINGS 5:1–9

The king thinks it's a setup. He thinks the king of Syria has sent this guy with leprosy and said, "You heal him. And if you don't heal him, I'm going to bring war." That's why the king tore his clothes.

Let's look at verse 9 again: "Then Naaman went with his horses and chariot," and in English it says "he stood at the door." But in Hebrew it says, "He stayed on his horse."

Naaman stayed on his horse, and Elisha did not walk out the door to greet him. Instead, Elisha sent a messenger to Naaman. The messenger came outside the house with Elisha's message. He said, "Go and wash in the Jordan seven times, and your flesh shall be restored to you, and you shall be clean" (v. 10).

Naaman became furious! He was well known as a mighty warrior. He was strong, smart, and victorious in battles—but he had spiritual arrogance. When Elisha's messenger told him what to do, Naaman got hot and went away and said:

> "Indeed, I said to myself, 'He will surely come out to me, and stand and call on the name of the LORD his God, and wave his hand over the place, and heal the leprosy.' Are not the Abana and the Pharpar, the rivers of Damascus, better than all the waters of Israel? Could I not wash in them and be clean?" So he turned and went away in a rage. And a servant came near to him and spoke to him and said, "My Father, if the prophet had told you to do something great, would you not have done it? How much more then, when he says to you 'Wash, and be clean'?" So [Naaman] went down and dipped seven times in the Jordan, according to the saying of the man of God; and his flesh was restored like the flesh of a little child, and he was clean.
>
> —2 KINGS 5:11–14

This is a phenomenal example of someone who almost missed the blessing of God—the blessing that would save his life. Why?

Because God didn't answer Naaman's prayer the way he thought God should.

DON'T LIMIT HOW GOD CAN DO IT

A lot of times we have a preconceived idea of how God is going to answer our prayer or meet our need. We think, "OK, God's going to do it, but He's going to do it this way."

When Naaman came to Elisha, he didn't get down off his horse. He didn't humble himself but actually expected special treatment from Elisha. Elisha refused to feed Naaman's desire to be noticed and admired, and he knew that the cause of his leprosy was pride. So Elisha kept him waiting outside and didn't come out.[2]

Elisha sent one of his disciples to tell Naaman the answer from God. The messenger said, "The master said that you're to go down and dip in the Jordan seven times."

Naaman got mad because he said to himself, "Here's how it's going to happen. Here's how I want You to do this, God. I want You to send Elisha out to me to wave his hand over me and heal the leprosy." But God didn't do it that way. The prophet said go dip in the river Jordan.

Instead of being thankful, Naaman was insulted. He said, "Why should I dip in there? Aren't there cleaner, more beautiful rivers to dip into?"

Notice that Naaman's servant understood his master's pride. The servant said to Naaman, "My father, if the prophet had told you to do something great, would you not have done it? How much more then, when he says to you, 'Wash and be clean'?" (v. 13). That was a wise servant!

So many times we miss what God wants to do for us because He doesn't do it the way we think He ought to do it. The Bible is full of examples like this. The question for you and me is this: Are we limiting God by telling Him how we think He should give us our miracle?

A WINESKIN OR A WATERPOT

Jesus, His disciples, and His mother all attended a wedding in Cana. If you recall the story from John chapter 2, Jesus' mother comes to Jesus and says, "We're out of wine."

Jesus replies, "My time has not yet come."

Mary, like a good Jewish mother, totally ignores Him and turns to the servants. Now pay attention to this! Listen to Mary's instructions. She tells the servers, "Whatever He says to you, do it" (v. 5).

Now why did she say that? Well, nobody knows, but I think she knew Jesus. She knew Jesus would tell them to do something that didn't make any sense.

Jesus says, "Go get me the waterpots used for the purifying of the Jews."

If those servants had been like you and me, we would have said, "Why get those? We already have wineskins. Jesus, You need to use the wineskins. It only makes sense, doesn't it? Yeah, I think it makes sense. Why would You want waterpots anyway?"

And that's what we do all the time. God says go do this. We reason, "Well, that doesn't make any sense. I have it figured out. God, here's how You need to do this."

Don't miss what God wants to do in your life because you have a preconceived idea that *this* is how He's going to do it. God doesn't need your wineskin to supply your need. There is no limit to what God can do, and there's no limit to how He can do it.

"Whatever He says to you, do it."

PETER'S FAITH DOES NOT LIMIT GOD

God enjoys meeting our needs with His miracles, but He often performs those miracles "outside the box," or outside what we consider normal.

I love the story of Peter's faith in the storm found in Matthew 14. Peter's habit was always to open his mouth and insert his foot. Peter was always getting into trouble. But Jesus loved Peter. I know that God doesn't love one person more than anybody else, but Jesus was both God and man, and I really believe Jesus loved Peter with a special love—not because Peter was doing everything wrong, but because he was always doing *something*.

In this story, Jesus' disciples are in a boat that is rocking from a severe storm. Suddenly, they see someone walking on the water, and they think it's a ghost.

But Peter says, "Lord, if it is You, command me to come to You on the water" (v. 28).

Jesus answered, "Come."

The story is not that Peter sank when he looked down. The real story here is that when he said, "Lord, command me to come," he walked on water. When Peter took his eyes off the Lord and looked at the storm, he started limiting what God could do and how he could do it—then he began to sink. But when he called back to the Lord, he walked on water again. The story is not the sinking, the story is the water-walking. Peter did walk on water by faith.

All the rest of the disciples stayed in the boat. It's *safe* in the boat. But it's also boring in the boat. You can either be a boat rider or a water walker. But the only way you can be a water walker is when you don't limit how God can do it.

MOSES' FAITH DOES NOT LIMIT GOD

Let's consider Moses. As Moses is leading the Israelites through the wilderness, he comes before God and says, "God, we're in the desert. We're dying of thirst. We need water." (See Exodus 17; Numbers 20.)

God says, "Don't worry. I have water."

"Whoa, thank You, Lord. What do we do?"

"Go talk to that rock."

Moses says, "You all stay here. I'll be right back."

It would be natural for God to open up the heavens and pour out rain. I'm sure when they asked for water, Moses was thinking God would send rain, or they would come over the next hill and see a lake or stream or river. But God's ways are not limited. God adds His *super* to our *natural*, and that's where we see the miracle take place.

If Moses had been like most Christians today, he would have said, "That doesn't make any sense. I'm not talking to a rock. God should have done it this way or that way."

No! Don't limit how God can answer you.

JOSHUA'S FAITH DOES NOT LIMIT GOD

I love the story of Joshua. After the death of Moses, Joshua is leading the Israelites into the Promised Land, but there's only one problem: the land is already inhabited, and the cities are fortified.

God tells Joshua, "Don't worry. I've given them into your hands." (See Joshua 6:2.)

Read the story. They're looking at the walls of Jericho. They see how thick they are, how high they are. What's more, the people living inside Jericho had enough provision to last them three years. The city was rich, stockpiled, and well protected with guards on top of this thick wall.

Joshua tells the people, "God has given us the city."

You and I would wonder if there were cannons coming or an earthquake about to happen—how would this wall come down?

God said, "Walk around the wall once a day for six days. On the seventh day, walk around the wall seven times. And when you're walking around, keep your mouths shut."

First day, nothing happens.

Second day, not even a crack.

Tuesday, nothing in the mail.

The seventh day comes, and they walk around that wall seven times—but keep their mouths shut. Why? Because death and life are in the power of the tongue. God told them to blow the trumpets but not to say a word. God knows the power in a person's tongue.

At God's command, after the final lap, when the priests gave a loud blast on their trumpets, all the people were to shout, and the walls would come down. I've been to the Jericho location in Israel. I've stood there where the walls came down. God brought them down.

I wonder, if they had been allowed to talk, how many people would have talked themselves out of the blessing on the seventh day?

Can God do anything? Yes. So don't limit how He can do it.

PETER DOES NOT LIMIT GOD AND PAYS TAXES

It's always Peter teaching us something in the Bible. Peter comes up and says, "Uh, Lord, I think I got us in trouble."

"What did you do now, Pete?"

"They came and asked me if we pay taxes, and I told them yes."

"Well, render unto Caesar what is Caesar's, and render unto God what's God's," the Lord replies.

Peter says, "I've got nothing."

"OK, well, go pay them."

"How do I do that?"

"Go fishing."

"No, Lord, You don't understand me. I need money."

"Go fishing."

Jesus knows that Peter likes to fish. So here's Peter going fishing, and he catches a fish. Right there inside the fish's mouth is a gold coin. (See Matthew 17:27.)

Imagine a friend walking by and his old fishing buddy says, "Hey Pete! What are you doing?"

"I'm going to pay taxes."

Now, why does God tell us these stories? Why does God give us these examples? The Bible says that our God is the same yesterday, today, and forever. Don't limit how He can do it. Don't limit God.

LIVING BY FAITH IS FUN AND ADVENTURE FILLED

Recently, Tiz and I were talking about living by faith and not limiting God. It's such a fun and adventure-filled way to live. It's so much fun knowing that you don't have to figure it out.

If God says get out and walk on water, you're going to walk on water.

If God says a gold coin is coming out of a fish's mouth, it's going to come out.

If God says water is going to come out of a rock, it's going to come out of a rock.

If God says a little boy's loaves and fishes are going to feed thousands of people, then it's going to happen.

This is what Jesus means when He says come to Him as a little child. When our grandkids—our "sugars"—were little, they would ride to church with us. We brought the sugars to church with us recently. As we were driving there, they didn't say, "Excuse me, Sabba (Grandpa), is there enough petrol in the automobile for us to get there? Have you checked the tires?" No; they got in and just trusted that Mom and Dad and Grandma and Grandpa were going to get them there. That's what it means to come to God as a little child.

Yes, we're in a battle, and we're fighting the enemy, but the fight is fixed. The enemy is going down.

Tiz and I have fun living by faith, when we don't limit how God can bring us His miracle. And you can have fun too if you don't limit how God can bring you the miracle that you need right now.

CHAPTER 17

DON'T LIMIT WHEN GOD CAN DO IT

LARRY HUCH

BEFORE I GOT saved, I was a street fighter. I was in the gangs. When I got saved, God didn't take my manhood; He just sanctified it. It bears repeating here that from the days of John the Baptist until now, the kingdom of heaven suffers violence, and the violent take it by force. God wants you to become a violent Christian and run into the battle and win the fight. Faith does not mean there are no battles. Faith means learning how to fight so you win the battles.

Men can still be men, and women can be warriors, but you've got to get up and fight. Have ever seen a bully? Every dad has had this conversation with his son. We tell our sons, "I don't want you fighting. Don't fight. But if somebody's picking on you, take the first shot." You have to learn to fight.

If the devil doesn't think you're going to push back, he's going to bully you.

In my mind's eye, I see a spiritual fist of faith—a fist that will knock the devil out! The thing about a bully is that once you knock a bully down, he's not bullying you anymore.

USE YOUR MEASURE OF FAITH

Is anything too difficult for God? No. So don't limit what God can do or how He can do it. We must humble ourselves like a little child to receive from God. We don't want to be spiritually arrogant like Naaman and blow it. When God says to do something, do it. That's why Mary said, "Whatever He says to you, do it" (John 2:5).

Elisha sent his messenger to tell Naaman, "Go dip seven times."

"Why seven?"

"Because I said so."

How many of us ever said that to our kids? But why? Because I said so, and I know more than you know right now.

Think about this. How many people do you know who need a financial breakthrough? People come up to me all the time and say, "Pastor, would you pray for this?"

I say, "Are you tithing? Are you a giver? If you want to harvest, you have to have seed in the ground." We can pray all day long, but if there's no deposit, there's no return. That's just the way it works.

Someone says, "Pastor, I don't have any friends."

I say, "The Word of God says if you want to have friends, be friendly."

Someone says, "I feel depressed."

I say, "The Word of God says to rejoice in the Lord always. Always. Don't rejoice just when everything's going great. Rejoice always."

Use your measure of faith. Don't limit what God can do, and don't limit how He can do it. But there's more: don't limit *when* God can do it.

DON'T LIMIT WHEN GOD CAN DO IT

So many times we think it's an act of faith that we put a timetable on God, and when it doesn't happen the way we think or when we think, we give up in our faith. Most people drop the ball on the one-yard line.

Let's talk about the third finger in the fist of faith:

- Don't limit what God can do.

- Don't limit how God can do it.

- Don't limit when God can do it.

There is a great story that pertains to God's timing, and it's found in John 11. Let's look at that story from the Word of God:

> Now a certain man was sick, Lazarus of Bethany, the town of Mary and her sister Martha. It was that Mary who anointed the Lord with fragrant oil and wiped His feet with her hair, whose brother Lazarus was sick. Therefore the sisters sent to Him, saying, "Lord, behold, he whom You love is sick." When Jesus heard that, He said, "This sickness is not unto death, but for the glory of God, that the Son of God may be glorified through it."
>
> Now Jesus loved Martha and her sister and Lazarus. So, when He heard that he was sick, He stayed two more days in the place where He was. Then after this He said to the disciples, "Let us go to Judea again." The disciples said to Him, "Rabbi, lately the Jews sought to stone You, and are You going there again?"
>
> Jesus answered, "Are there not twelve hours in the day? If anyone walks in the day, he does not stumble, because he sees the light of this world. But if one walks in the night, he stumbles, because the light is not in him."
>
> —JOHN 11:1–10

I can just see the disciples looking at each other going, *What?* Sometimes we think of the disciples as these mighty patriarchs. We picture Peter, James, and John with white hair and the beard to match. No, these guys were some of the least likely to be chosen by God, and it took them a while to lay hold of things Jesus was teaching. I say this to encourage us. Let's go on with the story now:

> These things He said, and after that He said to them, "Our friend Lazarus sleeps, but I go that I may wake him

up." Then His disciples said, "Lord, if he sleeps he will get well." However, Jesus spoke of his death, but they thought that He was speaking about taking rest in sleep. Then Jesus said to them plainly, "Lazarus is dead. And I am glad for your sakes that I was not there, that you may believe. Nevertheless let us go to him."

—JOHN 11:11–14

WHY DID JESUS WEEP?

He wept! Now, let me stop right there. Perhaps you know this is the only story in the Bible where it is recorded that Jesus weeps. Why? Perhaps for one reason, Jesus is realizing that they're really not believing Him. They're not getting that there's nothing impossible with God.

Jesus is thinking, "If they don't get it that I can raise Lazarus from the dead, they're going to have a hard time when I'm killed and buried."

This is the whole reason behind the death and resurrection of Lazarus. God wanted people on earth to know that if He can raise Lazarus from the dead, then God can raise His own Son from the dead. Let's continue the story:

Then Thomas, who is called the Twin, said to his fellow disciples, "Let us also go, that we may die with Him." So when Jesus came, He found that he had already been in the tomb four days. Now Bethany was near Jerusalem, about two miles away. And many of the Jews had joined the women around Martha and Mary, to comfort them concerning their brother. Then Martha, as soon as she heard that Jesus was coming, went and met Him, but Mary was sitting in the house. Now Martha said to Jesus, "Lord, if You had been here, my brother would not have died. But even now I know that whatever You ask of God, God will give You."

Jesus said to her, "Your brother will rise again." Martha said to Him, "I know that he will rise again in the resurrection at the last day." Jesus said to her, "I am the resurrection and the life. He who believes in Me, though he may die, he shall live. And whoever lives and believes in Me shall never die. Do you believe this?"

—JOHN 11:16–26

Jesus is teaching them, but they still aren't getting it. At least Thomas is faithful to Jesus. He's ready to die with Jesus since he insisted on going to a place where they want to kill him.

Yet Jesus is asking the most important question of our lives today. Do you believe that Jesus is the Son of God? Do you believe that Jesus is the resurrection and the life and that anyone who believes in Him, though he may die, yet will he live?

Let me take this one step forward. Maybe you are a mature Christian and you believe that God will resurrect your body after it dies, but do you believe that God will resurrect your dream?

LET GOD RESURRECT YOUR DREAM

Has the enemy, the world, or someone killed your dream? Has the enemy said, "It won't happen; it's too late; it should have happened four days ago or four years ago"?

Don't let anyone or anything kill your dream because today Jesus is the Lord of the resurrection. God can resurrect your dream.

Think about it. Jesus said, "I am the resurrection and the life. He who believes in Me, though he may die, he shall live. And whosoever lives and believes in Me shall never die. Do you believe this?" (John 11:25–26).

Do you believe this? Mary believed. Let's look at Mary's reply:

She said to Him, "Yes, Lord, I believe that You are the Christ, the Son of God, who is to come into the world." And when she had said these things, she went her way and secretly called Mary her sister, saying, "The Teacher has come and is calling for you."

—JOHN 11:27–28

Now I want you to see something here. It does not say that Jesus was calling her. Mary was in the house. You can almost see her grief-stricken or maybe even pouting, but Martha is feeling some faith, so she goes to Mary and tells a little fib. Martha says, "The Rabbi's calling you," because Martha wants Mary to get in on this. Maybe it's not too late. Maybe though Lazarus has been in the tomb for four days, maybe though it looks like our dream is dead, maybe the resurrection isn't going to take place *someday*—maybe the resurrection of our dream is going to happen *today*.

A RARE KIND OF FAITH

Are you ready for a resurrection of your dream today? Hallelujah! Let's continue our story:

> As soon as she heard that, she arose quickly and came to Him. Now Jesus had not yet come into the town, but was in the place where Martha met Him. Then the Jews who were with her in the house, and comforting her, when they saw that Mary rose up quickly and went out, followed her, saying, "She is going to the tomb to weep there." Then, when Mary came where Jesus was, and saw Him, she fell down at His feet, saying to Him, "Lord, if You had been here, my brother would not have died."
> —JOHN 11:29–32

I want you to get this: to walk in the kind of faith that God wants you to walk in is a rare thing. Jesus is right there in front of them, in the flesh. He's taught them and performed miracles. Martha served Jesus a plate of food in her home, and Mary washed His feet with the oil and her hair. Even these close friends of Jesus could not attain the faith for their miracle. Their reaction was, "If You would have been here four days ago, our brother would not have died."

The disciples weren't getting it. Mary and Martha weren't getting it. Nobody was getting it. To have this kind of faith is a rare, rare thing. But God will give you this kind of faith if you'll realize there is no limit to *what* He can do, there is no limit to *how* He can do it, and there is no limit to *when* He can do it. Even if it looks like it's dead, Jesus is the Lord of the resurrection.

Do you believe that Jesus is the resurrection and the life? Can Jesus' resurrection touch your dead dream and bring it to life? I hope you're shouting, "Amen!"

HANG AROUND WITH FRIENDS OF FAITH

John 11:33 says, "Therefore, when Jesus saw her weeping, and the Jews who came with her weeping, He groaned in the spirit and was troubled."

Let me say something about faith—a key to your faith. Watch out who you hang around with. When Jesus saw her weeping, thinking it was too late, and the Jews who came with her were weeping, thinking it was too late, Jesus groaned in the spirit and was troubled.

> And He said, "Where have you laid him?" They said to Him, "Lord, come and see." Jesus wept. Then the Jews said, "See how He loved him!" And some of them said, "Could not this Man, who opened the eyes of the blind, also have kept this man from dying?"
>
> —JOHN 11:34–37

Jesus wept because of their unbelief.

Have you ever heard the saying "Misery loves company"? Listen, I love everybody. I'll pray with everybody, but I don't hang with everybody. I don't want to hang with someone who loves to drain you. You say something good, and they'll say, "Yeah, but—"

You say, "Man, don't you love living under the blue skies?"

"Yeah, but—"

"Don't you love when it rains?"

"Yeah, but—"

There's always a person around who's got the "yeah, but." Don't hang with that person, because misery loves company. Now, you can't choose whom you're related to, but you can decide who you hang out with. And you want to hang out with those who love God and live in faith.

Jesus saw everyone else weeping, and Jesus wept. He must have been so frustrated. He must have been thinking, "Don't you understand? You've seen Me heal blind eyes. You've seen Me heal the lepers. You've seen these miracles. Why do you still not believe?"

And here we have the shortest verse in all the Bible, "Jesus wept" (John 11:35).

Then the Jews around them said, "See how He loved him" (v. 36).

Jesus was sad because, "According to your faith be it unto you" (Matt. 9:29, KJV).

FAITH IS A DECISION

Everyone has a measure of faith. It's important to build up positive faith—not negative faith. Faith is a decision. God says this to us right now:

- Is anything too hard for the Lord?

- Can I do it any way I want to?

- Can I do it any time I want to?

Have you made your decision? Have you said yes to those three questions?

Don't limit when God can do it. John 11:37 says, "And some of them said, 'Could not this Man, who opened the eyes of the blind, also have kept this man from dying?'" Do you see how logic starts getting in? They were thinking, "Well, He opened blind eyes, but He couldn't heal the man from dying?"

Jesus felt their unbelief and grief, but He made a decision. Look what it says.

> Then Jesus, again groaning in Himself, came to the
> tomb. It was a cave, and a stone lay against it. Jesus said,
> "Take away the stone."
>
> —JOHN 11:38–39

TAKE AWAY THE STONE

My friend, take away the stone. Take away the limitations. Take
away the limitations that block the blessing and the resurrection.
That's what Jesus is saying. *You* take it away.

Now, it's the same Lord that's going to raise Lazarus from the
dead, but He wants you to partner with the resurrection. You go
up there and remove the stone. You go up there and stop saying
negative things, stop thinking negative things. Stop limiting
God in what He can do. You go up—and do it today. Go up and
decide, "I'm removing the stone so my dream, my future, can
be resurrected in Jesus Christ." It's your part of the partnership
with God.

Let's watch this miracle unfold:

> Jesus said, "Take away the stone." Martha, the sister of
> him who was dead, said to Him, "Lord, by this time
> there is a stench, for he has been dead four days." Jesus
> said to her, "Did I not say to you that if you would
> believe you would see the glory of God?" Then they took
> away the stone from the place where the dead man was
> lying. And Jesus lifted up His eyes and said, "Father, I
> thank You that You have heard Me. And I know that
> You always hear Me, but because of the people who are
> standing by I said this, that they may believe that You
> sent Me." Now when He had said these things, He cried
> with a loud voice, "Lazarus, come forth!" And he who
> had died came out bound hand and foot with grave-
> clothes, and his face was wrapped with a cloth. Jesus
> said to them, "Loose him, and let him go."
>
> —JOHN 11:39–44

Martha thought it was too late because Lazarus' dead body would stink after four days. Please know this:

- God is never too early.

- God is never too late.

- God is always right on time.

We wonder why Jesus didn't come early and save Lazarus from dying? Jesus wanted to build their faith because He was about to die too. It would take faith to wait three days for Him to rise again. What's more, Jesus knew that after He ascended into heaven, He would leave the kingdom in their hands. Were they ready to believe God for all He wanted to do? Were these first Christians from the first church ready to partner with God?

FAITH FOR TODAY

Jesus plainly said, "Whoever lives and believes in Me shall never die" (John 11:26). That's you and me too. Like Jesus said to Martha, "Do you believe this?" If so, then you have the victory necessary to overcome the world.

> And this is the victory that has overcome the world—our faith. Who is he who overcomes the world, but he who believes that Jesus is the Son of God?
> —1 JOHN 5:4–5

This is the last of the last days, and it's such an exciting time to be alive. And guess what? God is looking for people in His kingdom today who have faith to lay hold of His plans.

God has a spiritual kingdom, and the only hands He can leave it in are those who don't limit *what* He can do, *how* He can do it, and *when* He can do it. God enjoys working together with His family, and since faith moves the mountains in front of us, God has to leave His kingdom in the hands of people of faith. Are you hearing what I'm saying?

FAITH PRODUCES PATIENCE

It takes patience and forcefulness to press in and take the kingdom of heaven. Mary and Martha had to be patient to see their brother alive and well again. It took forcefulness to roll away the stone and faith to believe Lazarus would come forth when Jesus called him. Mary and Martha and their friends endured a test of their patience and a trial of their faith, but Jesus came through with their miracle!

> My brethren, count it all joy when you fall into various trials, knowing that the testing of your faith produces patience. But let patience have its perfect work, that you may be perfect and complete, lacking nothing.
>
> —JAMES 1:2–4

Patience is one of the fruits of the Spirit. If someone says they are filled with the Spirit of God, but they don't have patience, they're not filled with God's Holy Spirit. They may have some of the Spirit, but not the fullness of the Spirit.

I wouldn't pray for patience, and I surely wouldn't pray for a trial! You get what you request from God, so be careful what you pray for! But when you encounter a trial in your life, or you're in a battle, count it all joy! Just remember, if you believe God, then the fight is fixed.

Patience has a perfect work, but a lot of times we think of the word *perfect* as meaning flawless—that we should be absolutely flawless without even a sniff of sin in our lives. That's not what *perfect* means. The word *perfect* in Hebrew is *tamim*. And *tamim* describes a situation in which you're completely out of ideas. In this verse, that's what the word *perfect* means. Let patience have its perfect work. You're out of ideas, and you're wondering, "How am I going to do this? I have tried everything that I know to do." When you've run out of ideas, God will bring the miracle and you will see a perfect work.

I'm sure with Lazarus they tried everything. I'm sure they gave him medicine. I'm sure they prayed. I'm sure they did everything they knew to do, but they ran out of ideas and Lazarus died. It's not how smart we are or how clever we are or how intelligent we are. There's nothing wrong with those things, but when we run out of ideas, we are wide open to see the supernatural power and resurrection of Jesus Christ!

NOAH WALKED WITH GOD

God loves to walk with us! God looks for people who will believe Him so He can work together with us to perform His miracles and His wonders on the earth. Even more than that, God enjoys our friendship. Let's see what the Bible says about Noah's testimony:

> Noah was a just man, perfect in his generations. Noah walked with God.
>
> —GENESIS 6:9

God walked with Noah side by side, face-to-face. Now, we know Noah wasn't a flawless man, but Noah believed God, and he and God had gotten to the point that they walked and talked face-to-face.

Several people who truly walked with God made it into the Bible. Noah, Moses, and Enoch all have the testimony that they walked with God. God went so far as to call Moses his friend!

> So the LORD spoke to Moses face to face, as a man speaks to his friend.
>
> —EXODUS 33:11

Enoch walked with God for years, side by side and face-to-face, until one day Enoch walked up the mountain with God and right off this earth and into the kingdom of heaven.

> And Enoch walked with God; and he was not, for God took him.
>
> —GENESIS 5:24

I love to study each person who walked with God, but it's fascinating to look at the life of Noah, especially when you consider that Jesus said in the last days the world will be like it was in the time of Noah.

> And as it was in the days of Noah, so it will be also in the days of the Son of Man: They ate, they drank, they married wives, they were given in marriage, until the day that Noah entered the ark, and the flood came and destroyed them all.
>
> —LUKE 17:26–27

Noah was not flawless, but he walked with God and was mature in his faith in God. Most of us know the story of Noah, beginning in Genesis 6.

Can you imagine what Noah went through? How long did Noah work on the ark? Some people say it took sixty to seventy years to build the ark, and others say up to 120 years. Let's say it was sixty years. Back in the days of Noah, it never rained. The earth was watered in the mornings by the dew. And here is Noah building a boat on dry ground.

The first week, Noah's neighbors come by and say, "Noah, what are you doing?"

"I'm building a boat."

"Cool! What's a boat?"

Noah preached to the people in his neighborhood. In fact, in 2 Peter 2:5, Peter calls Noah a preacher of righteousness.

Noah is building this huge boat with his sons, and he pauses to warn the people, "It's going to rain. It's going to pour. It's going to flood. You've got to get ready. Get your heart right with God!"

But then a month goes by. Two months go by. A year goes by.

The neighbors walk by and say, "Hey Noah, how's the rain coming?"

Ten years go by. Twenty years go by. Fifty years go by, and Noah is still sawing away, hammering away, building this ark. Talk about patience! Why did Noah keep building an ark all that time? He kept building because God said to do it. Noah does not know what rain looks like, and he keeps preaching to everyone to turn to God because rain is coming.

Noah doesn't know how God's going to do it or when God's going to do it, but he knows that God will send rain because God said it.

This kind of faith pleases God. Even though the world was wicked and violent in Noah's time, Noah believed God, walked with God, worked with God, and in essence restarted the human race. How? By faith in God's plan!

My Early Faith Testimony

I shared with you in a previous chapter how we needed $400,000 for a down payment to buy land for our building in Portland, Oregon. In short, we had three days to get the money in. But you don't go to the gym and lift seven hundred pounds if you've not been to the gym in twenty years! Just as your muscles would have to develop, my faith had to develop too. I want to share with you a testimony of faith that happened during my early walk with God.

Before Tiz and I were married, I was in a church in Flagstaff, Arizona. As a young disciple of Christ, I remember sitting in a service when suddenly God spoke to me. At the time, I loaded trucks and drove semis for a living.

The church was having a revival, and since I worked the evening shift, I took my lunch hour and came over to be in church, all dirty from work. I had just gotten paid. As I sat in the service, they took the offering, and God spoke to me and said, "Put the whole check in."

Remember, Jesus' mother, Mary, said, "Whatever He tells you to do, do it." To Joshua and Caleb, God said, "Walk around the wall seven times." They walked around the wall seven times. If God says dip seven times, dip! If He says, "Speak to the rock," then speak to the rock! It doesn't make sense, but that's OK. Just do whatever God tells you to do. Right?

I got paid every two weeks, so this check was fairly substantial for me back then. I thought, "God, I can't do that. I have rent on Monday."

Flagstaff is a college town. The house I was renting was owned by a guy who was notorious for being shrewd. Everyone knew that if you didn't pay your rent at the very moment it was due, he would take your deposit and rent out your house to someone else, because people were lined up in a college town to rent a house.

I said, "Lord, I've got rent."

God said, "Put it in."

"Lord, I'll put it all in but fifty dollars because I need the fifty dollars to add to what I have to pay the rent."

God said, "Put it all in."

So I signed a check and put it all in. Now, I would love to tell you that I went back to work and finished my night shift and the boss said, "Hey, you know what? I was just walking along, and I feel like I need to give you a hundred dollars." God can do that, but He didn't do it. I have to admit, the next day I got up, went to the mailbox, opened it up, and went through all the mail—and no money was there. I was thinking, "OK, Lord, when I go to church, You're going to speak to somebody at church, and they're going to walk up and say, 'Larry, I was praying, and God told me to give you fifty bucks.'"

I went to church on Sunday and nothing happened. Monday morning I got up, went to the mailbox, and nothing. Now, my rent was due at three o'clock on Monday, and I was still fifty bucks short. And I knew this guy—he was notorious. He was going to take my deposit, I was going to be out on my ear that day, and he would have my home rented by the next day.

I also worked in a school right across from my house, and I happened to be working that Monday at the front desk. I never worked at the desk, but for some reason they put me at the front desk that day.

So I'm thinking, "Lord, come on. What are You going to do? Come on. I'm fifty bucks short."

At about noon the mailman comes by and drops off the mail.

He says, "Hey, Larry. How are you doing?"

He leaves. I know his mail route. He goes up the hill and then comes back and hits my house about 4:30, which would be an hour and a half too late for me to pay my rent.

About a minute later the mailman comes back and says, "Hey, I'm running kind of late today. I just saw your mail in the back of my bag. You want it now?"

I said, "Yeah."

So he gave me my mail, and I opened it up. There's a letter from my Aunt Helen, the one who prayed me into the kingdom of God. She's the one who didn't look at the drugs and the drug addiction and the police record. She didn't look at any of that. She just believed God was going to save me. The letter came from St. Louis to Flagstaff, so it had to be put in the mail at least a day before I obeyed God.

My aunt said, "I was praying, and I felt you needed this."

Inside was a check for fifty-five dollars. Now, I needed fifty bucks for my rent, and the check was for fifty-five dollars. I needed fifty-five because 10 percent of that check belonged to the Lord! Let patience have its maturing, perfect work, and walk face-to-face with God, knowing that He is almighty God.

I know that those early tests and miracle provisions were God's way of training me to learn faith and faithfulness, which has continued to this day, forty-seven years later. My step of obedience and faith then put me on a path that has grown and multiplied beyond my wildest dreams and cemented into my core that we cannot over-trust or out-give our God! Life presents continual opportunities to choose to trust God and His promises and see and experience His endless realms of supernatural blessings and miracles!

YOU'RE NOT TOO OLD

God is going to do greater things than you've ever seen before, but you have to walk face-to-face with Him, not doubting. Be "perfect" and mature in your faith. The steps of a righteous man or woman are guided by the Lord.

- Don't limit what God can do.
- Don't limit how God can do it.
- Don't limit when God can do it.

If you are reading this and you are an older person, you may think, "Well, my time is gone. I'm too old now." Think about Joshua and Caleb. Because of other people's lack of faith, Joshua and Caleb missed out on forty years of their blessing in the Promised Land. It wasn't their fault—it was the unbelief of the people around them!

Forty years later God told them to lead the people into the Promised Land—not to mention that walk around the walls of Jericho. Joshua and Caleb said, "God, give me my Promised Land."

It's not too late! Read this prophetic word:

> So I will restore to you the years that the swarming locust has eaten, the crawling locust, the consuming locust, and the chewing locust, my great army which I sent among you. You shall eat in plenty and be satisfied, and praise the name of the LORD your God, who has dealt wondrously with you; and My people shall never be put to shame.
>
> —JOEL 2:25–26

If you have a dream for God to use you, God says in His Word that He restores the years that the locust and cankerworm have eaten.

Maybe you're wondering, "How can God restore the years?"

Well, He can't give you forty years back, but He can take all the blessing, all the harvest, all the joy, all the prosperity that was supposed to be yours for those forty years, and He can multiply it and bring it all now. I'm telling you, Joshua, I'm telling you, Caleb, your best years are still to come!

YOU'RE NOT TOO YOUNG

If you are a young person reading this book, I want you to listen carefully to this prophetic word because it is just for you. Don't let the devil come in and say, "You're too young to serve God right now. You know what? When you get older you can do this or do that for God."

Jesus is the same yesterday, He is the same today, and He will be the same tomorrow. (See Hebrews 13:8.) God says, "Let no one despise your youth" (1 Tim. 4:12). That means don't let anyone put you down just because you are a young person or a young Christian.

What has God put in your heart? Do you want to be a prophet of God, a businessman or a businesswoman? Let God place His desires in your heart, and don't let anybody come and say that it won't happen for you. Don't let doubt convince you that you're too young.

The apostles were young men. The disciples were young men, and the Bible says they shook the world. Esther was a young woman, and she stepped up to the plate and put her life on the line. She was totally committed when she told the people, "If I perish, I perish" (Est. 4:16). Esther saved the entire nation of Jews at that time. Young person, if you will not limit God, He will use you to shake the world.

Old or young, it doesn't matter who you are. Male or female, white, black, or brown, God has a destiny for you that is exceedingly, abundantly above anything you can ask or think.

Don't limit what God can do, don't limit how God can do it, and don't limit when God can do it!

I'd like to address another aspect as to why Jesus wept. Our Savior was God in the flesh. He was also a human on earth who experienced all the emotions, hardships, rejection, pain, and heartaches that you and I experience. Hebrews 4:15 tells us that we have a high priest who is touched by the feeling of our infirmities. Jesus, the Son of God, endured the cross and gave His life for you, me, and the world. Not only does He have sympathy for what we go through. He has empathy for us because he has been there too. Consider the following.

Jesus wept.

Jesus knew Lazarus was dead before He arrived. But He still wept. He knew Lazarus would be raised from the dead and alive again. But still He cried. He knew death here in the natural is not forever. Yet He wept. Jesus experienced personally that the world is full of pain, loss, suffering, sadness, disappointments, and devastation. His friends were heartbroken, and He felt it, and He wept. He wept because even when we know the end of the story, we can still cry at the sad parts because we have a tender, caring heart.

My family and I have learned and experienced that standing in strength and faith doesn't mean we don't feel the heartache and realities of what is going on within us or around us. Many times during this journey, I would get emotional trying to give updates to our families, friends, and congregations. As a man, I tried to stay strong for my family and our people but heard so often that people appreciated seeing the raw emotions and feelings that we were going through. Even though we know everything is going to turn out for the good, it is still OK to cry and express emotions at times.

CHAPTER 18

DON'T LIMIT WHOM GOD CAN USE

LARRY HUCH

D O YOU NEED a miracle? Do you need an answer to prayer? Remember, God can use anybody!

If we are going to live by faith, then we don't want to limit what God can do, how He can do it, or when He can do it. It's equally important that we don't limit through whom God can do it.

Many times, people miss the blessing because they think God's going to do things a certain way, or they think God's going to use a certain person. There is no limit with God. He can bring your miracle through anyone or anything!

GOD DOES NOT SEE AS MAN SEES

Of course, we are human, and we tend to look at outward appearances. We often say it's important to make a good first impression, so we dress up for job interviews or look the part for whatever work we apply to do.

God looks past our outer appearance and sees deep inside our hearts. God sees if we are in faith or doubt, fear or love. He knows if someone is walking in arrogance or humility. He sees if a person truly loves Him or just wants to get something from Him. If a person complains all the time, God knows that too.

That's what Psalm 103:7 means when it says, "He made known

His *ways* to Moses, His *acts* to the people of Israel" (MEV, emphasis added). Moses was a friend of God, and God opened His heart to Moses and showed Moses His ways. The children of Israel complained, grumbled, and even blamed God when they faced hardship. They demanded food, water, and victory over their enemies. God acted on their behalf by sending water from a rock and manna from the sky, but only those like Joshua, who sought God's presence, actually came to know God Himself and God's ways.

In an earlier chapter, we read from 1 Samuel 16 the story of David. It's amazing that David was the least in his father's house, yet God saw David's heart and sent the prophet Samuel with a horn of oil to pour over David and commission him the next king. Not only was David destined to be the next king of Israel, but out of his lineage would come the Messiah, the Christ. What a promise from God!

But before Samuel met David, he told Jesse he wanted to see his sons. Of course, Jesse brought out his eldest son. Eliab was tall and handsome and looked pretty impressive before Samuel. Let's read what God thought at this moment in history:

> So it was, when they came, that he [Samuel] looked at Eliab and said, "Surely the LORD's anointed is before Him!" But the LORD said to Samuel, "Do not look at his appearance or at his physical stature, because I have refused him. For the LORD does not see as man sees; for man looks at the outward appearance, but the LORD looks at the heart."
>
> —1 SAMUEL 16:6–7

I mean, this guy Eliab looked like a king. You see, many times, we miss what God is doing because we miss the package in which God is bringing our miracle.

GOD CAN PACKAGE YOUR MIRACLE ANY WAY HE WANTS

We picture these great and powerful apostles with white hair and white beards. Paul was a little red-haired, freckled, bow-legged guy. We tend to think a miracle has to be somehow magnificent, but in reality, God can package His miracles in any way He sees fit.

One of the amazing things we read in Scripture is in Hebrews 13:2, when God says in essence, "Watch how you treat strangers because you may be entertaining an angel." That angel may be old, young, white, Black, or Hispanic. That angel may be tall or short. You never know. What God is saying is, "Don't limit the package in which I can bring you your miracle."

GOD PACKAGES HEALING MIRACLES DIFFERENTLY

When Tiz and I pray for people who need healing, we ask them, "What does the doctor say?"

A lot of times, they will say, "Well, I won't go to the doctor. I'm trusting God. I'm not taking the medicine. I'm trusting God."

This is a familiar story, and it's kind of corny, but it illustrates what I'm trying to convey here. A guy's in a flood. The river floods his house. He's up on the rooftop, saying, "God, help me! God, help me!"

A guy comes by in a canoe, and he says, "Get in. I'll take you to shore."

The guy on the rooftop says, "No, no. I'm trusting God."

The guy in the canoe goes away. Now the water's up to the man's knees, and he's saying, "God, help me! God, help me!"

A guy in a motorboat comes by. He says, "Get in. I'll take you to shore."

"No," the man replies. "I don't need your help. I'm trusting God."

Now the water's up to the man's neck, and he's still on the rooftop, yelling, "God, help me!"

A helicopter comes and lowers a rope. The person inside says, "Grab the rope. I'll pull you up, and take you to shore."

The man calls back, "No, I'm trusting God to help me." Then he drowns.

When he gets to heaven, he says, "God, why didn't You help me?"

God says, "Who do you think sent the canoe, the motorboat, and the helicopter?"

You see, God can package a miracle in many different ways. God can open the windows of heaven and pour manna out. God can cause a rock to gush water, but sometimes God wants you to go down to the river and catch a fish.

In Matthew 17, Jesus could have just given Peter the money to pay the taxes. But Jesus said, "Go catch a fish." Peter didn't say, "Well, this isn't the way I expected Jesus to answer me." He did as Jesus instructed, and he caught a fish with a coin in its mouth for him to use to pay taxes for himself and Jesus (vv. 24–27). Many times, we expect a miracle to come in some lightning-bolt way, and sometimes it will happen that way. But sometimes our answer comes in a very subtle way, and that is no less miraculous.

God could wave His hand and heal us, but He may choose to give a doctor the wisdom needed to provide the treatment needed for your body to be healed. You're still healed either way. Who cares how the miracle comes?

NAAMAN'S HUMBLE MESSENGERS

In chapter 16, I shared the story of the healing of Naaman, who had been stricken with leprosy. If you recall, the first person who brought him the answer he needed was a slave girl. The real miracle is that this slave girl had been kidnapped from Israel during a raid Naaman led. This little girl was taken from her family in Israel and forced to serve Naaman's wife. The girl could have harbored bitterness and resentment against Naaman and his wife, but instead she shared with him what was basically the gospel in his day: "There is a God in Israel, and Elisha is His prophet." There is no record that this little girl was rewarded for pointing Naaman to God, yet this girl who believed God for her master's healing is one of the few children mentioned in the Old Testament.

Naaman went to the king, and the king wouldn't help him. But Elisha learned of Naaman's request and told him to come to him. When Naaman arrived at Elisha's house, Naaman sat up on his high horse and expected Elisha to come to him. Instead, Elisha made him wait, and then sent his messenger to tell him, "Go and wash in the Jordan seven times, and your flesh shall be restored to you, and you shall be clean" (2 Kings 5:10). Instead of doing as the prophet instructed, Naaman went away mad and nearly missed his miracle. But one of Naaman's servants said, "If the prophet had told you to do something great, would you not have done it? How much more then, when he says to you, 'Wash, and be clean'?" (2 Kings 5:13). Naaman expected Elisha to come out and wave his hand over him and heal him, but God had a different method in mind.

Naaman thought, "Surely we have better rivers where I'm from than here." If God was going to have him wash in a river, why not choose one of the rivers of Syria? They were mighty waters compared to the Jordan. The river Jordan looked like a creek next to the larger rivers of that day. But God likes to give us what we don't expect, and then see if we will have the faith to receive it. When Naaman dipped seven times in the Jordan, just as Elisha said, he was healed.

ORAL ROBERTS AND THE RACETRACK OWNER

Do you believe the Bible when it says the wealth of the sinner is laid up for the righteous? Years ago when Tiz and I were having dinner with Oral and Evelyn Roberts, I asked Oral Roberts about a story I'd heard about him and a guy who owned a racetrack.

Oral immediately knew what I was referring to. He said he needed $5 million at the time, and this guy who owned a racetrack gave him the $5 million. Oral told me, "When I said [publicly] that this guy gave me $5 million, my donor base dropped in half."

Good Christian people seriously questioned Oral's decision to take money from a racetrack owner, a sinner who presumably advocated gambling. But Proverbs 13:22 says the wealth of the sinner is laid up for the righteous. God will transfer wealth from the camp of the wicked to the camp of the righteous.

Before the racetrack owner's gift, people were saying, "Oh, Brother Roberts, we're believing God. We know God can do it." Then God spoke to an unlikely person to meet Oral's financial need, and Christians didn't like the vessel God chose to use.

Someone once asked me, "Pastor Larry, would you take the devil's money?" I replied, "The moment that money's in my hand, it ain't the devil's money no more! That's kingdom money."

OUR $20,000 MESSENGER

Remember in a previous chapter I wrote about a woman who brought us $20,000 at the eleventh hour? I didn't tell you all the details of that story because I wanted to save one part for this chapter.

If you recall, we were down to twenty minutes before the bank would close. We got a phone call, and a woman on the other end said, "I'm moving to Seattle, and I'm in Vancouver. But God told me to give you a check for $20,000, and I can't leave until I bring it to you."

The woman drove all the way back to where we were. We had twenty minutes left when she pulled into the parking. The thing I didn't tell you before is that when she handed me the check, she said, "I know God told me to give this to you because I don't even like you."

I grabbed the check and said, "But I love you!" I'm not joking. The woman didn't like the faith message. She didn't like our church being multicultural, but she couldn't leave town until she obeyed God.

We had been praying and praying for God to give us a miracle. When this woman said, "Well, here's the money, but I don't even like you," I could have chosen not to take it. But had I done that, I would have missed the miracle. I would have been like the man who drowned on the rooftop because he refused to recognize all the ways God answered his prayer. We have a tendency to get so religious that we miss what God's trying to do because the package is not wrapped in the way we think it should be wrapped. Look, if you are reading this book and you don't like me but God is telling you to send me $20,000, I love you. That may sound funny, but I'm not joking!

RELIGIOUS PEOPLE CAN BE MEAN

When I first got saved, I'd been working at this place where everybody knew I was a drug dealer and a drug addict. Then all of a sudden, I got saved and came back to work, saying, "Guess what, everybody? I got saved."

An older woman who was very religious said, "What denomination?"

I said, "The one with Jesus." That's all I knew. Then I began to tell her my testimony.

She said, "Oh, do they speak in tongues?"

I said, "Yeah, I got baptized in the Holy Ghost."

She replied, "Oh, no. We have to pray for you and get that out of you."

We limit God because of our religious background. We limit what God can do because it's not in the package we like.

SIX THOUSAND KIDS SAVED IN THREE YEARS

I remember when Tiz and I started our church in Santa Fe, New Mexico. We went out and saw six thousand kids saved in three years. God blessed our ministry. We just loved everybody. We led outreaches and were witnessing on the streets all the time. We had kids living with us. We opened girls' homes. We were just doing what we sensed the Lord leading us to do. But because I wasn't raised in religion, I didn't know how mean religious people could be.

Here we were pastoring this church in Santa Fe, where all these kids were getting saved. I mean, we had gang members coming to Christ. The courts were sentencing juveniles to Tiz and me.

A judge in Albuquerque called me one time and asked, "Is this Reverend Huch?"

I had never been called reverend in my life, but I said, "Yes, this is he."

He said, "I've got this young person. He's sixteen, and I have to either send him into a juvenile detention center or to you. I hear your program is the only one that's working. Can you come down and see him, Reverend?"

I said, "I'll be right down." They brought the kid to us, and God delivered him. He got set free, and he is in the ministry today. Praise God!

Our church was 98 percent Hispanic. My kids Anna and Luke spoke half English, half Spanish. That's the way they learned to talk. They didn't even know the difference. I'd come home and they'd greet me, "Padre!" That's because all their babysitters and everyone who took care of them spoke Spanish.

So all these gang members were getting saved. Then one day the head of the Catholic Church there said, "It's a mortal sin if your kids go down to that church. They will be excommunicated."

He didn't care that the kids were getting delivered of drugs. He didn't care that they were leaving the gangs behind. He just cared about religion. I'd never faced anything like that before. I'm a kid pastoring my first church in a liquor storefront in the neighborhood. I'm witnessing to homeless kids who are sniffing paint and living under a bridge.

Tiz and I were putting them up in our house. Then all of a sudden, the Grand Poobah was preaching against us. I didn't know what to do. I was devastated. I was praying, "God, show me what to do," because this guy actually got a petition to have me run out of town.

Then one Sunday morning, I arrived at church to find the blood and guts of some animal smeared all over the door of the church. I proceeded to preach that Sunday, and while I was preaching, I saw a vision. I saw people with candles, and I knew they were doing witchcraft against me. I'd never had a vision like that in my life. I felt way out of my league.

That afternoon, I went home and found our two parrot-type birds were dead. We had two dogs, and they were lying on the floor almost dead. A friend called around that time and said, "I'm praying for you. I just feel something isn't right."

I said, "Man, I don't know what I'm battling." I hung up the phone, thankful that God put it on someone's heart to pray.

God Speaks Through Babes

That evening, I was praying in our little apartment of about six hundred square feet. Tiz was in the bedroom ironing, and I was taking a bath. The whole while, I'm saying, "God, I don't know what to do. They're talking about throwing me out of town."

Our daughter Anna was three years old at the time. She was sitting in her high chair when all of a sudden she started screaming, "It's Jesus! It's Jesus! It's Jesus!" I mean, it was so electric with the anointing of God that Tiz came out of the bedroom. I jumped up and threw a robe on.

I said, "Anna, what are you talking about?"

She pointed to the corner and said, "Look, Dad. It's Jesus. Right there, it's Jesus. Do you see Him?" I was looking for a voice of God or for somebody with white hair and a white beard. I was looking for a man who's a prophet or a woman who's a prophetess. I was saying, "God, give me an answer. I don't know what to do." And all of a sudden, my three-year-old daughter is saying "Dad, right there. There He is. Do you see Him? Dad, look. It's Jesus!"

Then it came on me. I said, "Anna, did He talk to you?"

She said yes. So I asked, "What did He say?"

She looked at me and said, "Daddy, He told me to tell you, 'Preach His Word. Preach His Word.'"

My little three-year-old daughter delivered the answer from God I'd been crying out for! Psalm 8:2 says, "Out of the mouth of babes and nursing infants You have ordained strength, because of Your enemies, that You may silence the enemy and the avenger."

DON'T MISS YOUR MIRACLE MOMENT!

Don't miss your miracle moment because the package isn't what you expected. Sometimes the package wears a suit. Sometimes the package has flowing white hair. Sometimes the package has tattoos. Sometimes the package is a child. Sometimes the package is a doctor. Sometimes the package is your boss. Sometimes the package is a stranger.

Sometimes the package is white. Sometimes the package is Black. Sometimes the package is male. Sometimes the package is female. Sometimes the package is wise. Sometimes the package is educated. Sometimes the package is uneducated. But the miracle is still the same. Don't miss your miracle moment because you're expecting different packaging!

Are you believing God for a miracle? Let's pray together right now.

> *Father, in the name of Jesus, I release an anointing of faith on myself and on my friend reading this book. I thank You for Your gift of faith that has been distributed into our lives, and we promise that we will not limit what You can do. We will not limit how You can do it. We will not limit when You can do it. We will not limit the package in which You send this miracle. Father, in the name of Jesus, in prayer right now I cover my friend and myself with an anointing of faith that will never run dry, and I pray that we will grow*

*in this anointing of faith, and our faith will get greater
and greater and greater until the coming of the Messiah. I claim it in Jesus' mighty name. Amen.*

GOD'S "PACKAGING" FOR JESUS

When the Father sent Jesus to the earth, He placed His baby boy
in a feed trough in a stable. Prophets said Christ would come out
of Bethlehem, but no one pictured the King of glory being delivered to this world in a barn.

There's not a lot in the Bible about Jesus' childhood, but Isaiah
prophesied that the Christ would not be a tall handsome man
with charisma. Isaiah's prophecy tells us that Jesus was not the
best-looking lad in town.

> For He shall grow up before Him as a tender plant, and
> as a root out of dry ground. He has no form or comeli-
> ness; and when we see Him, there is no beauty that we
> should desire Him.
>
> —ISAIAH 53:2

When Jesus appeared on the scene publicly, more than one
person asked, "Can anything good come out of Nazareth?" They
asked this because Nazareth did not have a good reputation.

Could it be that God intentionally hid His precious treasure,
His only Son, inside packaging that no one was attracted to?

Today, religious people question Jesus' validity for the same
reason. They don't like the way they expect Him to look or the
way He calls us to repent and turn from our sins and receive
Him as Lord.

It's possible that you're reading this book but have never considered Jesus your personal friend and Savior. Tiz and I pray that
you don't ignore Him because of the package man or a denomination has wrapped Him in but that you receive Him because He
is wrapped in love. He is a gift to you from God the Father.

If you would like to receive God's greatest gift to you, then
pray this prayer out loud with us right now:

Father, I come to You right now, in the name of Jesus.
I know I've sinned. We've all sinned. You love me so
much that You sent Jesus Christ to pay the price in full
for all my sin. Right now, I receive Jesus Christ as my
Lord and Savior. Jesus, You died for me. Starting today,
I will live for You. In Jesus' name, amen.

If you prayed that prayer just now, then I want you to know that God's heart is rejoicing! He has desired that you would be His child since you were conceived in your mother's womb. Not only that, but Tiz is your sister, and I am your brother! We are family now. Send us an email at contact@larryhuchministries.com and let us know that you prayed to received Jesus today. And welcome into the family of God!

CHAPTER 19

DON'T LIMIT FOR WHOM GOD CAN DO IT

LARRY HUCH

D O YOU BELIEVE God is going to give you the miracle
you need? Do you believe Jesus is able to do the thing
you're asking Him to do?

Remember, Romans 12:3 says God has dealt to each one a
measure of faith. So every one of us has a measure of faith from
God, and every one of us can do our part to develop our faith.

In Matthew 9, we read about when Jesus touched the eyes of
two blind men who had been following Him around, crying out
for mercy. Jesus asked them, "Do you believe that I am able to do
this?" They said, "Yes, Lord." Jesus touched their eyes, and then
He said a remarkable thing: "According to your faith let it be to
you" (Matt. 9:27–29).

ACCORDING TO YOUR FAITH— POSITIVE OR NEGATIVE

Now think about this. God has predestined you to be successful. I'm going to show you that in the Word of God. None
of us is predestined to fail. We are predestined to be more than
conquerors, but because of situations and circumstances and
not understanding God's Word, that faith you have sometimes
becomes negative.

It's important that we understand that when Jesus said,

"According to your faith let it be to you," He was not just saying, "According to your positive faith be it done to you." If you have negative faith and believe, for instance, that God has it in for you and is going to bless someone else and not you, then you'll receive according to your negative faith.

I know we've discussed this already, but I've found that I need to think about these things a few times in order to grasp them. If you recall, God told Moses and the people of Israel that He had given them land. When the Israelites went to scout out the Promised Land, ten of the spies came back and said, "The land is beautiful and lush, but the people are strong, and the city is fortified, and we'll die trying to claim it."

And God said, "As I live...just as you have spoken in My hearing, so I will do to you" (Num. 14:28). We live in a negative world. We're around negative people all the time. But God says you are more than a conqueror, and you can walk in great faith.

MY DOG STORY

Years ago, when Tiz and I and the kids were pastoring in Spokane, Washington, we lived near a guy who was breeding and training German shorthaired pointers. These dogs were selling for $8,000 to $10,000 apiece. At that time, we were making a hundred dollars a week as pastors—if we got paid at all. So I would just go out there and look at these dogs and watch the man train them because I love to be outside.

Another guy told me about a friend of his who ran the Humane Society, and he said there was a German shorthaired pointer there. I went down there and looked at the dog. Then I bought it for fifteen dollars and took it to show the guy training German shorthaired pointers.

When I arrived, there were a bunch of rich guys out there who had paid $8,000 to $10,000 for their dogs and were now having them trained for six months. I'd been watching this going on for some time. I pulled in to the place, and my dog got out of the car and pointed by freezing its body.

The breeder and trainer guy looked him over and said, "Where did you get this dog?"

I said, "The Humane Society."

He said, "This is a top-of-the-line dog."

I didn't pay $10,000; I paid fifteen dollars.

Remember, nothing is too difficult for God.

1. Don't limit what God can do.

2. Don't limit how God can do it.

3. Don't limit when God can do it.

4. Don't limit through whom God can do it.

In this chapter, I want to share a fifth point: don't limit for whom God can do it. If you think my dog story is a good one, wait until you hear what God did for my son, Luke!

LUKE'S DOG STORY

Back in those days in Spokane, we were pioneering a church, and we had a Wednesday night service in our home with thirty to fifty people coming every week. That's not all. Tiz and I had two other families living with us and the kids.

One was a Hispanic family we had taken in whose husband had abandoned her and their three kids. So we let her and her three kids live in the middle floor of our house. There also was an ex-drug addict whom we'd led to the Lord off the streets. She had a little boy and her disabled father, so we put them in the upstairs bedrooms to get them off the streets. All three families shared the house. Tiz, our kids, and I lived in the basement, with all four of us sleeping in one bed.

Our son, Luke, was four years old at the time, and he slept with his dog, Banjo. Luke loved that dog. Banjo went with him everywhere.

Well, one Wednesday night when everyone was arriving for the service, somebody opened the door and Banjo ran out. I didn't notice that Banjo was gone until one of the guys ran into the house and got me. He said, "Pastor, you've got to come here."

He took me into the garage, where Banjo was laying. He had been run over and dragged for a mile down the road before the driver stopped. I was out in the garage thinking, "Oh my goodness, this dog's dead. Banjo's not going to make it." There was blood everywhere, and he was unconscious and barely breathing.

Right away I said, "We've got to put this dog somewhere so Luke doesn't see it." All of a sudden Luke was there beside me, asking, "Dad, what happened to Banjo?"

I said, "Well, Luke, Banjo got run over."

Luke said, "Dad, pray for Banjo. Pray for him."

We did pray. We laid hands on Banjo, and that night everybody went to bed. I kept getting up all night to look in on Banjo because this great man of faith didn't want Luke to see Banjo when he died. But Banjo kept living. He didn't have blood coming out of his ears or nose; he actually looked like he had been crushed. So I had very little hope that he would survive. But remember what we've been talking about?

1. Don't limit what God can do.

2. Don't limit when God can do it.

3. Don't limit how God can do it.

4. Don't limit through whom God can do it.

5. Don't limit for whom God can do it.

So, Luke woke up the next morning and said, "Daddy, is Banjo going to die?"

I said, "Well, son, Banjo is really hurt."

Then Luke asked me, "Jesus won't let him die, will He?"

Oh, my! I said, "Luke, well…why don't you pray for Banjo?"

Let me tell you, I know animals, and this dog was all but gone. Luke laid his hands on the dog and said, "Jesus, I know You won't let my Banjo die, that by Your stripes, he's healed."

I'm not exaggerating when I tell you Banjo jumped up and started running around. He ran all over the place, drank all of his water, ate his food, and wagged his tail—I'm not joking. I pulled out my wallet and I said, "Luke, pray for my wallet!"

That is a story of childlike faith. So again, don't limit what God can do; don't limit how God can do it; don't limit when God can do it; don't limit through whom God can do it. But most of all, don't limit for whom God can do it.

The experience of Luke laying hands on Banjo and God miraculously healing Banjo has been a foundational faith miracle for forty years for our family. I am just now realizing the greater and far-reaching impact and significance of this for our family, especially for Luke. Who could have foreseen that Luke's childlike faith and prayer to heal his beloved Banjo, then God's miraculously raising him up, would translate out all these years later.

The same caring, almighty God that answered Luke's prayer as a little boy to heal his dog answered his prayer as a father to heal his seven-month-old baby boy!

NOW I CALL YOU FRIEND

You may believe God healed Banjo when Luke prayed. You may believe God can do miraculous things. But you think He'll do those things for other people and not for you. Understand that the devil doesn't care if you believe God can work miracles. What he doesn't want you to believe is that God will do it for *you*. The same God that did miracles for Luke's dog, Banjo; Lion; and Tiz wants to do miracles for you!

Remember the words of Jesus:

> This is My commandment, that you love one another
> as I have loved you. Greater love has no one than this,
> than to lay down one's life for his friends. You are My
> friends if you do whatever I command you. No longer
> do I call you servants, for a servant does not know what
> his master is doing; but I have called you friends, for all

things that I heard from My Father I have made known
to you.

—JOHN 15:12–15

Jesus is talking about covenant here. He's talking about loving
us one another, and that's a tremendous teaching. Jesus taught
that people will know we belong to Him when we love one
another. But let's take this a step higher. Jesus said, "Love one
another as I have loved you....You are My friends if you do whatever I command you. No longer do I call you servants."

Jesus was saying, "I don't care if you've come from prison, the
abortion clinic, drug rehab, Wall Street, or Washington, DC. I
don't care if you're from college or the streets. No longer do I call
you a servant, but now I call you a friend—if you obey the Lord."

What's the difference between a servant and a friend? Jesus
said a servant doesn't know what his master is doing, but a
friend is a confidant. You confide in a friend. Jesus reached a
point in His relationship with His followers that when the Father
spoke to Him, Jesus turned around and spoke that message to
His disciples.

We did not choose Jesus; Jesus chose us. You may argue that
God can't use you for this reason or that, but God chose *you*—
warts and all! God chose you to be born and walk with Him
in this moment in history. He appointed you to bear fruit that
will remain on the earth. Jesus realizes that we are going to have
needs, so He promises, "Whatever you ask in My name, that I
will do, that the Father may be glorified in the Son" (John 14:13).

GOD'S LOVE IS PERSONAL

We've seen in Scripture that God can bring water out of a rock
(Exod. 17:6), open blind eyes (Matt. 9:27–30), and pull a gold coin
out of a fish's mouth (Matt. 17:27), but where it gets down to the
nitty-gritty is when it comes to our personal life. We think, "Yes,
God can, but will He do it for me?"

Not only is the devil a liar, but he's the father of all lies (John

8:44). The devil will tell you God won't do something miraculous in your life because you're too young, you're too old, you're too male, you're too female, you're too this, you're too that, you don't have enough education, you have a bad past, you failed God before. The devil will always approach us with reasons God won't do something for us. He tells us we don't deserve it, but we do deserve it—not because of anything we've done but because Jesus made a covenant with His blood that no one can break.

I know it may seem hokey, but I want you to say this out loud because faith comes by hearing: "I deserve it. I deserve to be blessed."

The devil wants you to think you don't deserve to be blessed. And on our own merit, we don't. But through the merit of Jesus Christ, we do deserve it. Remember, Jesus made a covenant with His blood that no man and no devil can break. Jesus loves us, and because of His love, you and I deserve to be blessed.

THE ACCUSER

Tiz and I started our very first church in Santa Fe, New Mexico, in a little liquor store that doubled as a meat market. What used to be Henry's Liquor Store was now our church, and it was down in the ghetto, where the drugs, gangs, and prostitutes were. That old, adobe building had about twenty-six leaks in it and one nasty little toilet. My office was the beer cooler. I'm not joking! We've come a long way, as I'm sure you have too. Don't limit who or what God can use, right?

There was a guy who would come in while Tiz was playing the organ. She knew three chords, and I'm so glad she did! I led worship, and this guy would come in and sit down. As soon as we finished singing and I started to preach, this man would get up, go to the back door, and just stare at me all mean in the face. Then he'd leave. This went on for a couple of months. He'd come every Sunday, and I could never get to him. He came in late and then left early, but before he left, he always gave me that dirty look.

One week I had a friend preaching for me, so as we were singing the last song, I thought, "I'm going to grab this guy." But the man saw me coming and bolted for the door. I ran after him out the back door and down the street, the whole time calling out to him, "Sir, sir, wait a minute! Wait a minute! Where are you going?"

Finally, he stopped and turned around, and said, "You have no right." Then he began to name all these things in my past. "You have no right," he said again. "If these people knew your past, if they knew your background..."

It didn't dawn on me until later, but he said things only I, God, and the devil knew. The Bible says Satan is the accuser of the brethren (Rev. 12:10). Satan is the one who brings up the past.

As I started to walk away, I thought, "I don't deserve to be a pastor." Just then, the Lord grabbed me inside and said, "Don't you ever let somebody bring up what has been covered in the blood of My Son, Jesus. Don't you let him bring it up."

Don't be surprised if when your faith becomes stronger and you know God can do it, the devil shows up with that still, small voice of hell and begins to tell you, "You don't deserve it." He is a liar!

BIBLICAL COVENANT

We do deserve God's blessing and God's best because we have a covenant with almighty God through the blood of Jesus Christ. Many of us don't understand biblical covenant. People on the streets understand covenant more than people in the church.

This is a terrible illustration, but every streetwise person will know this. When you're on the street with a gang, you're fighting me, and I'm fighting you. But when "the man" (the police) comes, we stand with each other. That's a covenant code of the street.

I hate to say this, but being a liar is accepted in our society now. If you are around my age, you remember when people could call you this or that, but if they said, "You're a liar," they'd just started a fight! Why? Because when I was young, it meant something to be a man or woman of your word.

Today we're not surprised when a politician lies. I'm not saying all politicians lie, but a lot of politicians do. It's just the way people are in our society. People lie and cheat. They're unfaithful to their spouses, and they keep getting caught and still don't change. We see it in movies and on television, and it's become like the proverbial frog in the pan. We've gotten so used to people not being men and women of their word that we hardly flinch when another "scandal" hits the news.

It used to be that we didn't have to make contracts four hundred pages to cover every little thing, but nowadays you have to guard yourself. There was a time when you went into a courtroom, put your hand on the Bible, and said, "I promise to tell the truth, so help me God." A person's word used to mean something. If I tell you I'm going to do something, you can take me at my word and know I'm going to do it. You can count on the fact that I'm not a liar. This is what a covenant is all about.

Nowadays, we don't really have covenants; we have contracts. And as I mentioned, when you draw up a contract, you have to cover every little thing because people will lie and cheat and steal and bend and twist trying to get ahead. In reality, if you and I come in agreement, if we shake hands, that's it. We're in covenant. No papers signed. No nothing. If I say I'm going to do something, I'm going to do it. Even if it costs me, even if I make a mistake, even if it's a threat to me, I'm going to keep my covenant word.

We don't understand this today, but what Jesus is talking about in John 15:12–15 is not something to be taken lightly. Jesus is making a covenant with us through His blood. In other words, our bond with a brother and sister may be strong and real. But a blood covenant is more powerful than even a family relationship. Jesus made a blood covenant with you and me that is even thicker than what He had with His own earthly family. Jesus' blood covenant with you is thicker than anything, and it cannot be broken.

I want you to catch this because when the devil says, "Well, you don't deserve it," you need to know how to respond. You have a blood covenant with Jesus that cannot ever be broken. When the Lord said, "I will never leave you nor forsake you" (Heb. 13:5), He was talking about a blood covenant He made with us that cannot be broken. Jesus said whatever you ask the Father in Jesus' name, He will give it to you (John 14:13). That is the covenant you and I enter into when we receive Jesus' blood as atonement for our sins.

God does still want us to be faithful to our families when we join in covenant with Him. However, when Jesus was told that His mother and brothers were outside waiting to talk to Him, He replied, "Who is My mother and who are My brothers?... Whoever does the will of My Father in heaven is My brother and sister and mother" (Matt. 12:48, 50). Jesus wants to cut a covenant with those of us who are in the will of the Father.

DAVID AND JONATHAN IN BIBLICAL COVENANT

One of the greatest examples of biblical covenant is David and Jonathan. The Bible says in 1 Samuel that David and Jonathan made a covenant.

> Then Jonathan and David made a covenant, because he loved him as his own soul. And Jonathan took off the robe that was on him and gave it to David, with his armor, even to his sword and his bow and his belt.
>
> —1 SAMUEL 18:3–4

What does this mean? Jonathan was the heir to the throne of his father, King Saul. But by taking off his robe and armor and giving it to David, Jonathan was saying, "Because of the blood covenant I make with you, David, I put you before my throne. I put you before my life. I put you before my father."

In Bible times, if two people made a covenant, the first thing they would do is face each other. They would look at each other face-to-face and then exchange robes. David had the robe of a shepherd boy, and Jonathan had the robe of a prince. They exchanged robes, which meant, "Now my authority is your authority."

Remember, God does not look on outward appearances but at the heart. These two young men each had powerful authority. David refused King Saul's armor, but he killed a giant in that shepherd's robe.

When Jonathan gave David his weapon, he was saying, "David, my father may be against you, the world may be against you, but I stand with you, and my army shall be your army."

Speaking of an army, do you remember that we are surrounded by a great cloud of witnesses (Heb. 12:1–2)? Right now, as part of your covenant as a child of God, there also are millions of angels positioned and ready to come to the aid of the heirs of salvation! You are not on your own. No weapon formed against you shall prosper. You are more than a conqueror, not because of your own strength, but because of the armies of heaven. Hallelujah!

EXCHANGING ROBES WITH CHRIST

When Jesus died on the cross, the soldiers took His robe and tunic and rolled dice for it. It is a sign of covenant that Jesus said, "You may have been a drug addict, you may have been a sinner, but I am taking My robe, My holiness, and I am giving it to you. I am offering My robe to anyone in the world who believes Me, and I am exchanging authority."

Your new covenant means you have Jesus' robe and Jesus' inheritance. You are a joint heir with Christ. Jesus is saying to us: "Wherever you go, I'm going with you. Every place you put the sole of your feet, I'll give it to you for an inheritance. Everything you put your hands to do is blessed." (See Matthew 28:20; Hebrews 13:5–6; Deuteronomy 11:24; Joshua 1:3; and Deuteronomy 30:9.)

EXCHANGING WEAPONS WITH CHRIST

The second thing that happens when a blood covenant is cut is that the two people would exchange weapons. Jesus said on the cross, "Do you think that I cannot now pray to My Father, and He will provide Me with more than twelve legions of angels?" (Matt. 26:53). But instead of calling a legion of angels, He allowed the soldiers to take a spear and pierce His side, and out of that wound came blood and water. Jesus laid down His weapon. He could have called a legion of angels, but He allowed the weapons of the earth to pierce His side. That spear was ours, and Jesus took it.

The weapons of our warfare are not carnal, but mighty in God (2 Cor. 10:4). And whatever you bind on earth is going to be bound in heaven, and whatever you loosen on earth is going to be loosed in heaven (Matt. 16:19). Because of this, I can declare, "Devil, I rebuke you. Death, I bind you. Stubbornness, I rebuke your hold. I loose the blessing of God." Friend, give your covenant a voice! Jesus died so we could live.

THE COVENANT SACRIFICE

After exchanging weapons, each person or community making a covenant would bring a sacrifice. Jesus died for us so we could live for Him. In covenant, we are to give our lives as a sacrifice to God.

> Present your bodies a living sacrifice, holy, acceptable to God, which is your reasonable service.
>
> —ROMANS 12:1

The beauty of our covenant with God's Son is that the more we give of our lives, the more He opens the windows of heaven and pours us out blessings.

So each man or each community would bring a sacrifice. A bull would be sacrificed on one side, and another bull would be sacrificed on the other. They would kill the bulls, and as the blood would shed, they would stand together in that blood and walk around the sacrifices in a figure eight. Why? Because on Yom Kippur, the Israelites would shed the blood seven different times, and that would break every curse. When Jesus died on the cross, He shed His blood seven different times. When Jesus was on the cross, He said in essence, "Not only is every curse broken, but now you are connected to eight, to new beginning. Now you are walking in covenant, in a supernatural walk with God."

The Eight Walk of Covenant

Eight is the number of new beginnings. Eight is the number of moving into the supernatural. When cutting a blood covenant, the two parties walked around the sacrifices eight times.

Are you ready to take your walk? Are you ready to walk in the power of God? Are you ready to walk in the blessing of God? Are you ready to walk in the anointing of God? Are you ready to walk in the favor of God? Are you ready to walk in the abundance of God? I believe God is healing marriages as you read these words. I believe people are beginning to move in the gifts of the Spirit as the Lord moves in their lives. God is bringing signs, wonders, and miracles for you and for me!

The Blood Covenant Hand

The parties entering into a blood covenant exchanged robes, they exchanged weapons, they gave the sacrifice, and they walked in a figure eight, saying this is now a supernatural new beginning. But then each person would take a sword or knife and slice his hand. They would literally cut a covenant. One person would cut himself, the other would cut himself, and then they would clasp hands, and the blood would mingle, indicating they were now blood brothers. They were saying, "My power is your power; my strength is your strength; my wealth is your wealth; my army is your army; my authority is your authority."

The blood covenant handgrip helps us fully understand these verses from the Word of God:

See, I have inscribed you on the palms of My hands.

—Isaiah 49:16

You shall also be a crown of glory in the hand of the Lord, and a royal diadem in the hand of your God.

—Isaiah 62:3

The Lord has sworn by His right hand and by the arm of His strength.

—Isaiah 62:8

And I give them eternal life, and they shall never perish; neither shall anyone snatch them out of My hand. My Father, who has given them to Me, is greater than all; and no one is able to snatch them out of My Father's hand.

—John 10:28–29

The soldiers didn't just tie Jesus to the tree; they nailed Him to the tree. That wasn't an everyday occurrence. There weren't nails everywhere for people to routinely have nails driven through their hands. It's not a coincidence that Jesus had nails driven into His hands because He was fulfilling prophecy. When His blood mixes with your blood, it's not your strength anymore, but by the might of His right hand that you shall be saved. (See Psalm 138:7; Isaiah 41:10.)

In Bible days, while the wound on their hands was healing, they would take ash from the fire and mix it in the wound, which would cause the wound to turn black. And if that person was traveling down a road alone and the enemy came, he would look at his scar and remember that he's not alone.

Here comes debt.

Here comes sickness.

Here comes divorce.

Here comes an attack on your kids.

Here comes the enemy, and it looks like he's bigger than you.

It looks like he outnumbers you. It looks like he's stronger than you. But you can hold up your hand and say, "It may look like I'm alone, but I am not alone. I have an army behind me. I have a covenant partner behind me."

I pray you lay hold of this revelation of your covenant with Jesus, the Son of God. When the devil comes against you, the devil will say, "Don't you know I'm bigger than you? Don't you know I'm tougher than you? Don't you know I'm better than you?"

But you lift up your hand and say, "You've got to understand I am not alone. I am in blood covenant with Jesus Christ, the Son of the living God. It may look like I'm alone, but greater is He that's in me than anything you can bring my way."

A COVENANT IN BLOOD IS FOREVER

Jonathan and David cut a covenant. That covenant was not for just a moment. A blood covenant is forever. There came a time when King Saul swore to kill David, but David survived. And then came a time of war, and Saul and Jonathan died. Jonathan had a son named Mephibosheth.

Here is Mephibosheth's story in a nutshell:

> Jonathan, Saul's son, had a son who was lame in his feet. He was five years old when the news about Saul and Jonathan came from Jezreel; and his nurse took him up and fled. And it happened, as she made haste to flee, that he fell and became lame. His name was Mephibosheth.
>
> —2 SAMUEL 4:4

Saul and his family told Jonathan's son, Mephibosheth, "David hates you, and David's in power now. If he finds you, he'll kill you." They fled the palace when they found out Saul and Jonathan died on the battlefield. The nurse was running down the palace stairs and fell, causing Mephibosheth to injure himself in a way that made him lame.

Please get this: Because Saul told his family David hated him,

Jonathan's son Mephibosheth was afraid David would kill him after David became king. That's what the devil does. He'll tell you God doesn't care about you. He'll tell you God hates you. He'll tell you God is looking at your failure. He'll tell you God is looking at your shortcomings.

Yet because of David's covenant with Jonathan, when David learned that Jonathan had a son still living, he began to look for him, not to kill him but to bless him!

God is looking for you too.

> For the eyes of the LORD run to and fro throughout the whole earth, to show Himself strong on behalf of those whose heart is loyal to Him.
>
> —2 CHRONICLES 16:9

The Bible says David had his servants bring Mephibosheth into what was now his palace. Jonathan's son was probably thinking, "He's going to kill me." But that's not what happened.

> Now when Mephibosheth the son of Jonathan, the son of Saul, had come to David, he fell on his face and prostrated himself. Then David said, "Mephibosheth?" And he answered, "Here is your servant!" So David said to him, "Do not fear, for I will surely show you kindness for Jonathan your father's sake, and will restore to you all the land of Saul your grandfather; and you shall eat bread at my table continually."
>
> —2 SAMUEL 9:6–7

David told him, "Before you were even born, you were royalty because of the covenant I made with Jonathan." The covenant didn't stop with Jonathan.

Before you were born, Christ died for you. Before you ever knew it, God made a covenant. Before you ever loved Him, He first loved you. You are not cursed; you are a prince or princess and joint heir with Christ Jesus. Do you get it? You were not ordained to fail. You were not ordained to lose. You were not ordained to be sick or in poverty. You were ordained to walk in victory as a child of God.

David told Mephibosheth in essence, "Before you were born, you were the beneficiary of a covenant promise that made you a prince." I started thinking about that—all those years I was a drug addict, all those years I walked in anger, all those years. Yes, I was born in South St. Louis, but before I was even born, God Almighty made a covenant with me.

When Lion and Tiz got sick, we immediately turned to our covenant with our Lord and declared: "You turned the intended curse into a blessing because you love me" (Deut. 23:5). "Christ has redeemed me from every curse, sickness and plague" (Gal. 3:13).

TALK TO THE HAND

The world has told you that blessings and miracles are not for you because of the color of your skin, or because you're male or you're female, or because you're too young or too old, or because you're not smart enough or you don't have enough faith. Those voices will always be around to tell you why you can't have God's best.

Do you know what you do? You say, "Go talk to the hand."

Is your marriage in an impossible situation? Talk to the hand.

Are your children away from God? Talk to the hand.

Is there anger, division, and discord in your family? Talk to the hand.

Are you weighed down by discouragement, anxiety, or hopelessness? Talk to the hand.

Do you struggle from financial or economic challenges? Talk to the hand.

Do you need someone to respect your authority? Talk to the hand.

Is the devil accusing and condemning you right now? Definitely tell him to talk to the hand.

You are more than a conqueror with God's equipping, favor, grace, and strength. No weapon formed against you will prosper.

Are medical tests showing a negative report or that death is at the door? Talk to the hand.

Have the world and people given up hope on you? Talk to the hand.

Do you lack confidence, self-esteem, or a sense of value? Do you feel alone and rejected? Talk to the hand.

You may be facing a huge, seemingly insurmountable health issue as we did with Lion and Tiz. Absolutely nothing is impossible for our God!

Just as we did, talk to the hand!

If you are ready for your covenant walk and your new beginning, pray this with me:

> *I am going to begin to walk in my covenant with God Almighty, and I am going to walk in the power of God. I am going to walk in the blessing of God. I am going to walk in the anointing of God, the favor of God, and the abundance of God. My marriage is going to be healed. My children are going to be godly men and women. I am going to move in the gifts of the Spirit, and see signs, wonders, and miracles. I say to all who rise up against me that you rise up against the armies of the living God. I declare to all who would oppose the plan of God for my life, "Talk to the hand!" Thank You, Jesus, for making a covenant with me! In the name of Jesus, the Son of God, amen.*

CONCLUSION
Tiz Huch

THE WRITING OF this book has been faith building, emotionally healing, and a celebration of so many victories for me in many ways. Oddly enough, the overriding feelings that arose within me were not of the horrific, dark emotional times or physical pain and suffering. The overriding feelings and memories have been of the incredible presence, provision, and power of the Holy Spirit I experienced each and every day! In the natural, it would make sense to feel a cloud of heaviness in looking back. To feel joy, peace, and sweetness is pretty astounding to me. Today, I can tell you that every morning I rejoice just to be able to get up and get on with life!

I am grateful that you've taken the time and effort to read this book. I am extremely proud of you for pressing in to all that the Lord has for you! God is supporting you and is with you each step of your journey. You are not alone.

Perhaps you are still in your season of trial. Hang on, my friend, and remember, for every mountain we face, our God has a miracle to overcome it. For every problem, He has a promise. For every disease, He has already provided our deliverance and miraculous healing. For every challenge, He has a triumph, and your victory is already in the works. No matter what issues we may face in our lives, God has a way through for us. As Romans 8:28 says, He is working *all* things together for our good!

SEE GOD IN YOUR PICTURE

I want to encourage you to pay attention to what you "see" in your inner soul. Remember, fear comes when we imagine our future *without* God in the picture. Faith comes when we imagine our future *with* God in the picture.

As I heard the oncologist's diagnosis that I had aggressive, stage 3 ovarian cancer, that familiar phrase came to my mind. Immediately, I chose to see my future with God in the picture. It made all the difference in my life. Now, in hindsight, I see the far-reaching effects this focus on God had on my life and on the miracles I experienced by the moment.

We have to guard our hearts from becoming depressed, discouraged, and cynical. It is easy to fall into the trap of accepting or expecting the worst. Do everything possible to picture yourself and your future on the victory side of your struggle. What will your future look like with God in the picture? I determined that although I had cancer, cancer was not going to have me! I was not turning over my identity and destiny to the big C. I was determined to be a *victor*. Saturating my soul with God's promises of healing was my number one priority. God, His promises, and His Word became my focus. I had to see myself healthy in my future.

My friend, put on faith. Put on victory. If you need to, fix yourself up by putting on fresh, cheery clothes. But most importantly, see God in your future. Faith comes when we see our future with God in the picture.

THE CHOICE TO REJOICE

Faith has a joyful, confident face. Faith and joy are married together. We've got this because God's got this! Philippians 4:4 says, "Rejoice in the Lord always. I will say it again. Rejoice."

Faith is not denying the reality of what's going on. Faith is denying your present reality the right to rule and reign in your life, family, health, finances, and future! Faith in our spirit means faith in our countenance and our attitude. The term *getting your game face on* applies not only in sports but in real life as well.

We don't bury our heads in the sand. We don't deny our difficulty and pretend it will just go away or that we can "faith" it away. We face that circumstance with faith and make the choice to rejoice because we trust in God's faithfulness, abilities, and almighty power. God's got this! "As your days, so shall your strength be" (Deut. 33:25). You rise up, and you overcome it. True spiritual joy and peace come from deep within our souls and are not contingent upon the current circumstances. They are solidified upon the foundation of our faith and trust in our God and His promises! Our confidence is not in ourselves. It is in our God! We can rejoice because we know He's got this!

You recognize those attacks that are coming against your family or your children, your marriage or your finances. You can't just walk away and pretend they're going to dissolve. That's not an active faith. Active faith is saying, "Oh, really? *Really?* You think you're going to come against *my* family? Not on my watch!"

Let me tell you, when cancer came marching into our lives, I had a righteous indignation rise up from within me. Deep inside I said, "No way!" I saw beyond just a sickness. I saw a spiritual attack—an attack that was trying to break the back of our family and break the impact of our lives and ministry. We did absolutely everything we needed to in the physical realm and then looked forward with the eye of faith—and there we saw our God in the picture. We saw our victory with God within us, surrounding us, and fighting for us!

We need to have bold, nonnegotiable faith. The Lord has a calling and an anointing on each of us to make an impact for Him. *Tikkun olam* means making the world a better place and helping broken lives. The happiest people I know are those who have discovered by chance or by choice that it truly is "more blessed to give than to receive" (Acts 20:35).

I want to encourage you to believe big and take the limits off God. Don't become weary or discouraged if your miracles take a while longer than you'd like. Be patient with the process. Embrace God's grace. Feed your faith. Walk in hopeful expectancy. Remember, God created Adam out of dirt. He loves to create something beautiful out of what appears to be commonplace.

FROM CATERPILLAR TO BUTTERFLY BREAKOUT

My favorite living illustration of godly hope is the transformation of a caterpillar into a butterfly. I love butterflies. I have displays of real butterflies all over my house and office. They are one of God's most beautiful, amazing creations. They are also a profound representation of the transforming grace and process of God.

When the lowly, earth-crawling caterpillar's life as it knows it is drawing to a close, it weaves itself a cocoon and goes into a deep sleep known as metamorphosis. In that dormant stage, the Spirit of God touches it. This little ground crawler grows wings. It wakes up but realizes it is trapped in its own cocoon. It pushes, struggles, and finally breaks free of the entrapment. As it struggles, its new wings gain strength and begin to spread. Suddenly, this beautiful, transformed creature emerges from the death cycle into a new life cycle and arises as one of God's most beautiful creations—a butterfly!

Sometimes we feel like caterpillars. We feel like our vantage point of life is the ground. We feel like we're just inch, inch, inching along at slow speed like a caterpillar. The caterpillar never imagined its life would be more than that of an ordinary ground crawler. Previously, it lived its life limited to a lowly view of itself and painstakingly crawling over and around obstacles.

Maybe you feel that way when suddenly God puts you in a little cocoon.

You say, "Nothing's happening here. I'm asleep. I'm missing out on life, and things are going on all around me."

Then you wake up and start to push and struggle to break out of the darkness and captivity. Through those very struggles, you become strong and gain the abilities to take flight.

I'm telling you, when you break out like that butterfly, you will know the transforming power and love of our God!

God has not destined you to the lowly existence of a caterpillar. He has destined you to be transformed and fly like a butterfly.

God has called you to accomplish every one of your dreams. It is my prayer that He will bless you greatly so that you can be an even greater inspiration, light, and blessing to all those around you.

In fact, I would like to lead you in this prayer over your life and future. I want you to picture yourself at the throne of God. Do not picture yourself at the throne of the mountain of problems. You're at the throne of God Almighty. When you come to Him, believe that He's already done what you're going to ask Him to do right now.

Just begin to press into Him, and when you feel God nudging you, lift your hands as you pray.

Read this prayer out loud, and enter in with me, OK?

Let's Rise Above in Prayer

Father God, thank You for Your love, kindness, mercy, grace, and salvation. I worship, honor, and praise You for how mighty, caring, and powerful You are.

Come into my heart. Make me a new person. Renew my heart, soul, mind, spirit, and body. Forgive me of all my sins and shortcomings. As You have given Your life to me, Jesus, I dedicate myself to You today and forever. I receive You into my life as my Lord and Savior, and I will serve You forevermore.

Father in heaven, I love You. I choose to rejoice in You, and I choose to be joyful. I choose to put a spirit of faith on the inside and the outside, and to trust You. But I am being real with You. I have issues in life. I have challenges that I face, Lord, and I am not ignoring those things—I am rising above them.

Father, right now I break every curse. I break every spirit of addiction. I repent of my sins. I break the grip and stronghold of the world's influence and the world's voices in my life, in my family's lives, in my children, grandchildren, and those You have given me to love in

*the world around me. I silence the world's voice and
its power through the blood and the authority of Jesus
Christ.*

*Father, I plead the very blood that was shed for me—
the blood of my Savior, Jesus. I plead that blood specif-
ically over my family, over my life, over the children in
my local schools, over my neighbors, over my community, and over my church. God, I break the strongholds
that would try to steal the hearts, minds, and souls of
my children and the children in my local community,
in the name of Jesus Christ.*

*Father, You are our healer. My God, I put my spiri-
tual foot down and declare: Nothing but the perfect
will and plans of God for me! Thy kingdom, perfection,
and dominion come, just as in heaven. Come into my
life; my mind, spirit, and body; my family; my finances;
my world; and my future in the name, authority, and
power of the Father, the Son, and the Holy Spirit. I
receive every one of Your blessings, promises, and
miracles by the moment! Thank You for blessing me
greatly so that I can be a great blessing, in Jesus' name.
I rejoice! Amen.*

ONE MORE PRAISE REPORT

I have one more praise report of God's perfect timing and restoration. In chapter 7 I told you that Larry and I were supposed
to greet Ethiopian Jews who were making aliyah to Israel on July
17, 2019. Because my emergency surgery was scheduled for the
same date, I wasn't able to go. I was so excited to meet these
precious people and celebrate their new life with them. We had
been working for so long to support the Operation Eagle's Wings
effort that I honestly felt robbed of this blessing. But our God is
not only a God of healing; He is also a God of restoration!

In July 2022 Larry, Katie, and I returned from a trip to Israel,
where the Israeli government and Karen Hayesod honored Larry

Huch Ministries with a very special award for our support for Israel, particularly our help toward aliyah efforts. In recent months we have helped over thirty thousand Ukrainian Jews displaced by the Russian invasion of Ukraine to immigrate to Israel.

On this trip in July 2022 we were able to meet many of these Ukrainian Jews, hear their stories, and get to know them personally. Coincidentally (though in Hebrew there is no word for *coincidence*), we also had the great pleasure of meeting an incoming plane of 160 new immigrants that we sponsored relocate to Israel. Guess where these people were from? Ethiopia! Guess when this took place? Almost exactly three years to the day we were supposed to meet the plane in 2019!

The enemy tried to take my life and rob me of my future and destiny. Three years ago when the oncologist diagnosed me with aggressive, advanced stage 3 ovarian cancer, my future flashed before my eyes—but I wasn't in it. That was a dreadful, fear-filled day when the reality hit that I might not live three more months, let alone three more years. But God! Not only did God save my life, but He restored my life! What the enemy tried to steal and destroy, my God restored and multiplied back to me and my family! The passion and labor of our lives was not destroyed or subdued. It has been thriving and multiplying! Rather than being diverted from our mission, we have become more focused and driven, and we have quadrupled our commitments!

Also, coincidentally, I made the final edits on this book during my flight home from that trip to Israel. What a confirmation of God's perfect timing, perfect plans, and perfect restoration! Only God could have arranged all this so perfectly!

We are blessed to be a blessing! When we are a blessing to others, the blessing multiplies back into our own lives. Rather than seeking to be blessed, seek to be a blessing. This is the key to living in realms of God's blessings, promises, and miracles by the moment!

God bless you greatly as you seek to *be* a great blessing!

101 HEALING DECLARATIONS

"PRAISE THE LORD! Bless the Lord, and all that is within me shall bless Your holy name! I will not forget Your benefits." This is the first prayer that bubbled up in me (Tiz) when the doctor reported I had cancer. These words from Psalm 103 overflowed from what I had planted in my soul in previous years. I declared that God had healed all my diseases, and I was healed and renewed. My friend, what God has done for me He is doing for you, and He has abundant goodness for you for such a time as this. He is on the throne, and your destiny is intact.

No matter what storm you are facing, look up to the face of God and declare these scriptures—out loud! Nothing is impossible with God, and you are more than a conqueror because of Christ, who loves us. Take every thought captive that would exalt itself above the Word of God, and purpose in your heart to envision His unlimited best for you. This is the list I pray every morning. Let these healing declarations soak in as you proclaim His promises. God will add His super to your natural as you walk into new levels of faith, healing, and restoration.

1. You are the Lord that heals me (Exod. 15:26).
2. My days shall be 120 years, and I will be in good health (Gen. 6:3; 3 John 2).
3. I shall be buried in a good old age (Gen. 15:15).
4. I shall come to my "grave in a full age, like as a shock of corn cometh in his season" (Job 5:26, KJV).

5. When You see the blood, You will pass over me, and the plague shall not be upon me to destroy me (Exod. 12:13).

6. You will take sickness away from the midst of me, and the number of my days You will fulfill (Exod. 23:25–26).

7. You will not allow on me any of the diseases that people fear, but You will take all sickness away from me (Deut. 7:15).

8. It will be well with me, and my days shall be multiplied and prolonged as the days of heaven upon the earth (Deut. 11:9, 21).

9. You turned the curse into a blessing for me because You love me (Deut. 23:5; Neh. 13:2).

10. You have redeemed me from the curse of the Law and from every sickness and plague; no evil shall befall me, and no sickness will come near my house (Gal. 3:13; Ps. 91:10; see also Deuteronomy 28).

11. As my days, so shall my strength be (Deut. 33:25).

12. You have found a ransom for me; my flesh shall be fresher than a child's, and I shall return to the days of my youth (Job 33:24–25).

13. You have healed me and brought up my soul from the grave; You have kept me alive from going down into the pit (Ps. 30:1–3).

14. You give me strength and bless me with peace (Ps. 29:11).

15. You will preserve me and keep me alive (Ps. 41:2).

16. You strengthen me upon the bed of languishing; You restore me in my sickbed (Ps. 41:3).

17. You are the health of my countenance and my God (Ps. 43:5).

18. No plague shall come near my dwelling (Ps. 91:10).

19. You will satisfy me with long life (Ps. 91:16).

20. You heal all my diseases (Ps. 103:3).

21. You sent Your Word and healed me and delivered me from my destructions (Ps. 107:20).

22. I shall not die, but live, and declare Your works (Ps. 118:17).

23. You heal my broken heart and bind up my wounds (Ps. 147:3).

24. The years of my life shall be many (Prov. 4:10).

25. Trusting You brings health to my navel and marrow to my bones (Prov. 3:8).

26. Your words are life to me, health and medicine to all my flesh (Prov. 4:22).

27. Your good report makes my bones fat (Prov. 15:30).

28. Your pleasant words are sweet to my soul and health to my bones (Prov. 16:24).

29. Your joy is my strength (Neh. 8:10). "A merry heart does good, like medicine" (Prov. 17:22).

30. "The eyes of the blind shall be opened" (Isa. 35:5). "The eyes of them that see shall not be dim" (Isa. 32:3).

31. "The ears of the deaf shall be unstopped" (Isa. 35:5). "The ears of them that hear shall hearken" (Isa. 32:3, KJV).

32. The tongue of the dumb shall sing (Isa. 35:6). "The tongue of the stammerers shall be ready to speak plainly" (Isa. 32:4).

33. The lame man shall leap as a deer (Isa. 35:6).

34. You recover me and make me to live. You are ready to save me (Isa. 38:16, 20).

35. You give power to the faint. You increase strength to them that have no might (Isa. 40:29).

36. You renew my strength. You strengthen me and help me (Isa. 40:31; 41:10).

37. To my old age and gray hairs, You will carry me, and You will deliver me (Isa. 46:4).

38. You bore my sicknesses (Isa. 53:4).

39. You carried my pains (Isa. 53:4).

40. You were put to sickness for me (Isa. 53:10).

41. With Your stripes I am healed (Isa. 53:5).

42. You heal me (Isa. 57:19).

43. My light breaks forth as the morning and my health springs forth speedily (Isa. 58:8).

44. You restore health unto me, and You heal me of my wounds (Jer. 30:17).

45. You bring health and cure, and You cure me and reveal unto me the abundance of peace and truth (Jer. 33:6).

46. You "bind up that which was broken, and...strengthen that which was sick" (Ezek. 34:16).

47. You cause breath to enter into me, and I shall live. And You put Your Spirit in me, and I shall live (Ezek. 37:5, 14).

48. Wherever the river comes shall live. I am healed, and everything shall live where the river comes (Ezek. 47:9).

49. I seek You, and I shall live (Amos 5:4, 6).

50. You have arisen with healing in Your wings (Mal. 4:2).

51. You said: "I will; be thou clean" (Matt. 8:3, KJV).

52. You took my infirmities (Matt. 8:17).

53. You bore my sicknesses (Matt. 8:17).

54. You are the Lord, my physician (Matt. 9:12).

55. You are moved with compassion toward the sick, and You heal me (Matt. 14:14).

56. You heal all manner of sickness and all manner of disease (Matt. 4:23).

57. According to my faith, be it unto me (Matt. 9:29).

58. You give me power and authority over all unclean spirits "to cast them out, and to heal all manner of sickness and all manner of disease" (Matt. 10:1, KJV; see also Luke 9:1).

59. You heal them all (Matt. 12:15).

60. As many as touch You are made perfectly whole (Matt. 14:36).

61. Healing is the children's bread (Matt. 15:26).

62. You do all things well. You make the deaf to hear and the dumb to speak (Mark 7:37).

63. All things are possible to me because I believe (Mark 9:23; 11:23–24).

64. When hands are laid on me, I shall recover (Mark 16:18).

65. Your anointing heals the brokenhearted, delivers the captives, recovers sight to the blind, and sets at liberty those that are bruised (Luke 4:18; Isa. 61:1).

66. You heal all those who have need of healing (Luke 9:11).

67. You did "not come to destroy men's lives, but to save them" (Luke 9:56, KJV).

68. You give me authority "over all the power of the enemy, and nothing shall by any means hurt [me]" (Luke 10:19).

69. Sickness is satanic bondage, and I ought to be loosed today (Luke 13:16).

70. In You is life (John 1:4).

71. You are the bread of life. You give me life (John 6:33, 35).

72. The words that You speak unto me are spirit and life (John 6:63).

73. You came that I may have life, and that I may have it more abundantly (John 10:10).

74. You are the resurrection and the life (John 11:25).

75. If I ask anything in Your name, You will do it (John 14:14).

76. Faith in Your name makes me strong and gives me perfect soundness (Acts 3:16).

77. You stretch forth Your hand to heal (Acts 4:30).

78. You make me whole (Acts 9:34).

79. You do good and heal all that are oppressed of the devil (Acts 10:38).

80. Your power causes diseases to depart from me (Acts 19:12).

81. "The law of the Spirit of life in [You] has made me free from the law of sin and death" (Rom. 8:2).

82. The same Spirit that raised You from the dead now lives in me, and that Spirit quickens my mortal body (Rom. 8:11).

83. My body is a member of You (1 Cor. 6:15).

84. My body is the temple of Your Spirit, and I will glorify You in my body (1 Cor. 6:19–20).

85. I rightly discern Your body, which was broken for me, and judge myself to be saved, healed, and delivered by You; therefore I will not be judged, I will not be weak, I will not be sickly, and I will not die prematurely (1 Cor. 11:29–31).

86. You have set gifts of healing in Your body (1 Cor. 12:28).

87. Your life is made manifest in my mortal flesh (2 Cor. 4:10–11).

88. You have delivered me from death, You do deliver me, and since I trust You, You continue to deliver me (2 Cor. 1:10).

89. You have given me Your name and have put all things under Your feet (Eph. 1:21–22).

90. You want it to be well with me, and You want me to live long on the earth (Eph. 6:3).

91. You have "delivered [me] from the power of darkness" (Col. 1:13).

92. "[You] will deliver me from every evil work" (2 Tim. 4:18).

93. You tasted death for me. You destroyed the devil, who had the power of death. You have delivered me from the fear of death and bondage (Heb. 2:9, 14–15).

94. You wash my body with pure water (Heb. 10:22; Eph. 5:26).

95. Lift up the weak hands and the feeble knees. Don't let that which is lame be turned aside, but rather let it be healed (Heb. 12:12–13).

96. Let the elders anoint me and pray for me in Your name, and You will raise me up (James 5:14–15).

97. As I pray for others, You heal me (James 5:16).

98. By Your stripes I was healed, and therefore I am healed (1 Pet. 2:24).

99. Your divine power has given unto me all things that pertain unto life and godliness through the knowledge of You (2 Pet. 1:3).

100. Whosoever will, let him come and take of the water of life freely (Rev. 22:17).

101. You wish above all things that I may prosper and be in health, even as my soul prospers (3 John 2).

NOTES

CHAPTER 1

1. "Elie Wiesel Quotes," AZquotes, accessed May 13, 2022, https://www.azquotes.com/author/15626-Elie_Wiesel.

CHAPTER 2

1. "What Is 'Ethics of Our Fathers'?" Chabad.org, accessed May 17, 2022, https://www.chabad.org/library/article_cdo/aid/680360/jewish/What-Is-Ethics-of-Our-Fathers.htm; Naftali Silberberg, "Why Is the Tractate Named 'Fathers'?" Chabad.org, accessed May 17, 2022, https://www.chabad.org/library/article_cdo/aid/517534/jewish/Why-is-it-Named-Fathers.htm.
2. "Tikkun Olam: Repairing the World," My Jewish Learning, accessed May 20, 2022, https://www.myjewishlearning.com/article/tikkun-olam-repairing-the-world/.
3. HaRav Avigdor HaLevi Nebenzahl, *Thoughts for Rosh Hashanah* (New York: Feldheim Publishers, 1997), 27.

CHAPTER 5

1. "Know, Knowledge," Bible Study Tools, accessed May 17, 2022, https://www.biblestudytools.com/dictionaries/bakers-evangelical-dictionary/know-knowledge.html.

CHAPTER 6

1. Eugene Peterson (@PetersonDaily), "All the water in the oceans cannot sink a ship unless it gets inside," Twitter, September 1, 2015, 9:49 p.m., https://twitter.com/petersondaily/status/638891341079007232?lang=en.
2. Leo Newhouse, "Is Crying Good for You?," *Harvard Health Publishing* (blog), March 1, 2021, https://www.health.harvard.edu/blog/is-crying-good-for-you-2021030122020#:~:text=Researchers%20have%20established%20that%20crying,both%20physical%20and%20emotional%20pain.
3. "Sermon Quotes: Loss," The Pastor's Workshop, accessed May 24, 2022, https://thepastorsworkshop.com/sermon-quotes-by-topic/sermon-quotes-loss/.

4. Jennifer Walsh, "Why Laughter May Be the Best Pain Medicine," *Scientific American*, September 14, 2011, https://www. scientificamerican.com/article/why-laughter-may-be-the-best-pain-medicine/.

CHAPTER 7

1. "Groups at Higher Risk for BRCA Gene Mutations," Centers for Disease Control and Prevention, September 27, 2021, https:// www.cdc.gov/cancer/breast/young_women/bringyourbrave/ hereditary_breast_cancer/higher_risk_brca.htm.

CHAPTER 11

1. Kaylena Radcliff, "A War Story: 'There Is No Pit So Deep God's Love Is Not Deeper Still,'" Christian History Institute, accessed June 30, 2022, https://christianhistoryinstitute.org/ magazine/article/there-is-no-pit-so-deep.

CHAPTER 13

1. *Merriam-Webster*, s.v. "aha moment," accessed July 5, 2022, https://www.merriam-webster.com/dictionary/aha%20moment.
2. *Merriam-Webster*, s.v. "awe," accessed July 5, 2022, https://www. merriam-webster.com/dictionary/awe.
3. *Merriam-Webster*, s.v. "awe."

CHAPTER 16

1. "Tzaraat—a Biblical Affliction," My Jewish Learning, https:// www.myjewishlearning.com/article/tzaraat-a-biblical-affliction/.
2. In the next few paragraphs I will be paraphrasing the account between Naaman, Elisha, and Naaman's servant found in 2 Kings 5.

ABOUT THE AUTHORS

LARRY AND TIZ Huch are the pastors of New Beginnings Church in Bedford, Texas, and hosts of the weekly television broadcast *New Beginnings With Pastors Larry & Tiz Huch*. Across forty-five years of ministry the Huchs have planted seven churches in the United States and Australia and written several books individually and together, including *10 Curses That Block the Blessing; Releasing Family Blessing; No Limits, No Boundaries; Free at Last: Breaking Generational Curses;* and *The 7 Places Jesus Shed His Blood*.

The Huchs are dedicated to building bridges of peace, friendship, and unity between Christians and Jews. To that end Larry Huch serves on the board of the Israel Allies Foundation and has received awards from the Knesset Social Welfare Lobby for helping to meet the needs of the Jewish people in Israel.

In February 2020 Pastor Larry received the Israel Allies Lifetime Achievement Award for his thirty years of support for the land and people of Israel. This prestigious honor was awarded by the Knesset Christian Allies Caucus at its thirteenth annual Night to Honor Our Christian Allies, an event to recognize Christian leaders who have been steadfast in their commitment to Israel.

Pastor Larry has been named twice to the prestigious Israel's Top 50 Christian Allies list, in 2020 and 2021. This coveted list includes Christian leaders from around the world who are staunch advocates for Israel.

Most recently, in 2022, Pastor Larry was selected as the first-ever recipient of the John Henry Patterson Guardian of Zion Award. This prestigious award was presented by Keren Hayesod to recognize Pastor Larry's steadfast support for and generosity to Israel and the Jewish people.

The Huchs have three adult children, a daughter-in-law, a son-in-law, and four grandchildren.